THE ENGLISH DEPARTMENT
IN A CHANGING WORLD

Open University Press

English, Language, and Education series

General Editor: Anthony Adams

Lecturer in Education, University of Cambridge

This series is concerned with all aspects of language in education from the primary school to the tertiary sector. Its authors are experienced educators who examine both principles and practice of English subject teaching and language across the curriculum in the context of current educational and societal developments.

TITLES IN THE SERIES

Computers and Literacy
Daniel Chandler and Stephen Marcus (eds.)

Children Talk About Books: Seeing Themselves as Readers
Donald Fry

The English Department in a Changing World
Richard Knott

In preparation

English Teaching: Programmes and Policies
Anthony Adams and Esmor Jones

Microcomputers and the Language Arts
Brent Robinson

Teaching Literature for Examinations
Robert Protherough

THE ENGLISH DEPARTMENT IN A CHANGING WORLD

Richard Knott

Open University Press

Milton Keynes · *Philadelphia*

Open University Press
12 Cofferidge Close
Stony Stratford
Milton Keynes MK11 1BY, England
and
242 Cherry Street
Philadelphia, PA 19106, USA

First Published 1985

British Library Cataloguing in Publication Data
Knott, Richard
    The English department in a changing world.—
(English, language and education)
1. English language — Study and teaching —
Great Britain
I. Title   II. Series
420'7'1041   PE1068.G5

ISBN 0–335–15033–0

Library of Congress Cataloging in Publication Data
Knott, Richard.
    The English department in a changing world.
(English, language, and education series)
Bibliography: p.
Includes index.
    1. English philology — Study and teaching (Higher)
I. Title.   II. Series.
PE65.K66   1985   428'.007'1173   85–317
ISBN 0–335–15033–0

Typeset by Marlborough Design, Oxford
Printed in Great Britain by St. Edmundsbury Press,
Bury St. Edmunds, Suffolk.

Contents

Acknowledgements

Thanks are due to many teachers whose ideas and experience have contributed to this book; they include:
Patrick Sanders, Bob Moy, Sophie Williams, Hilary Burton, David Curtis, Oonagh Cox, Kevin Head, Barry Smith, Paul Rhodes, Mick Connell, John Taylor HMI, Robin Curtis, Sandra Hann, Liz Gunner, Eva Tutchell, Jugal Sharma, Robin Richardson, Pete Allsop, Sylvia Hitch, Pauline Turner, Joan Ashton, Gavin Bolton, Gwyneth Bolt, Jean Lewis, Jacqui Dye, Debbie Reeves, Peter Anderson, Henry Hudson, Ron Price, Pennie Lambert, Stan Grue, Helen Vick, Colin Randerson
. . . . . .

General Editor's Introduction

This is an unusual book. The author is an English adviser and a former Head of a comprehensive school English Department and the book grows out of his concerns in in-service work with teachers on the running of English departments — in a context that makes increasing demands with dwindling resources.

At a time when the national climate is one that takes a more utilitarian and behaviouristic view of teaching in general it is particularly important to have a clearly articulated statement for English teaching which challenges this view. While adopting a resolutely realistic stance, Knott nonetheless takes an uncompromising position in his defence of the best that has been traditional in English teaching and in pointing the ways forward for the subject's future.

Such issues as the growth of microtechnology and its effect on literacy are taken on board sympathetically but with no mistaken idealism. Knott shows himself throughout well aware that English teaching, and teachers, cannot stand alone but must adapt to the changing world.

The book is particularly rich in the lists of resources that it provides (rather more practical and up-to-date than is often the case) and in the charts and tables that provide useful summaries of the argument presented in the chapters. It has deliberately been arranged so that it could serve as the basis of a departmental seminar for a serving English department — hence the series of topics for discussion and the simulation exercise with which it ends.

Richard Knott believes in the central role of talking and listening within the English curriculum and his book reflects this. Its form is one that seeks to open up discussion rather than one that is authoritarian in tone but it would be wrong to mistake this for a lack of authority in the writer. The style is part of the index of the message that the book presents: the reader is invited to enter into a conversation with the writer and with himself in the process of reading the book. This can as easily be done by the individual reader as by the reader working alongside others.

'The English Department in a Changing World' was written in the latter part of 1984 which makes it exactly contemporary with the DES/HMI document, 'English, 5–16'. It provides an admirable corrective to that document in reaffirming a holistic approach to English teaching which refuses to accept an atomistic approach that reduces English to a series of narrowly defined objectives. In this Richard Knott is very much in touch with the expressed views of many of his fellow

English advisers who will find a good deal to applaud in this book. It refuses to duck the basic issues of our times (see the chapter on evaluation for example) but it also makes no concessions to contemporary fashion when it is fundamentally inimicable to humane values in education.

The text is a personal statement of considerable and urgent importance. Its tone is accordingly a personal one, fleshed out with anecdote and particular examples, based on a practical as well as an intellectual understanding.

The Bullock Report — 'A Language for Life' — was published in 1975; it is appropriate that Richard Knott's book should be published exactly ten years later. Necessarily Bullock was the document of a committee, a generalised view of English teaching, however enlightened. The present volume puts flesh on the bones of Bullock, presenting a resurrection for which the world of English teaching has been waiting.

Anthony Adams

1 The Purpose of English Teaching

At the leaving age, many of our children are inarticulate; more are unable to express themselves on paper; and most remain unapprenticed to literature, that is to life. It was said by a writer of the last century, 'Our clowns are the stupidest in Europe. They can't spell; they can scarcely speak. They haven't a jig in their legs. And I believe they're losing their grin.'

The doom-laden comment is taken from W. S. Tomkinson's *The Teaching of English*, first published two years after the end of the First World War. The criticism levelled at teachers of English in the 1980s, however, still focuses on the gap seen to exist between the various aspirations of teachers on the one hand and the lack of preparedness young people are supposed to show when they leave school. It is salutary to ask children to reflect upon and articulate *their* perceptions of the teaching of English; they can present a bizarre view of the experience through which they have been passing:

English is to improve your vocabulary and to pronounce words well, also to recognise writers' works and speeches and to understand any meanings in them.

I see English as a subject where you learn all the basics in the first and second year, while in the third year you read a lot and study more English writers, e.g. Shakespeare.

Put that against what most teachers of English think they are teaching and there is clearly a no-man's-land over which the battle will rage! We have not articulated with any real success what the nature of 'English' is: not to the parents and employers who remember, most of them painfully, their diet of clause analysis, composition and corrections; still less to the children themselves – the messages about 'English' are confused. No doubt we would feel sympathy for the third-year girl who could write tentatively in her journal:

* My strength is imagination, but I have a weakness thereabouts; I am too shy to use it and write it down at school or in a school book. I find when I

do write, my imagination begins to wander and I have to watch what I am writing ... I think a teacher could help us to get over our shyness.

At fourteen, it would be nice to think that she had acquired a certainty about teacher response that made such doubts misplaced. However, it is more than likely that her view of what 'writing' is has been distorted by a variety of teachers pursuing their vision of what they deem good practice in English to be, supported by a hotchpotch of theories as to how 'language' works.

Figure 1   'A picture of the possible interpretations of English as a subject'

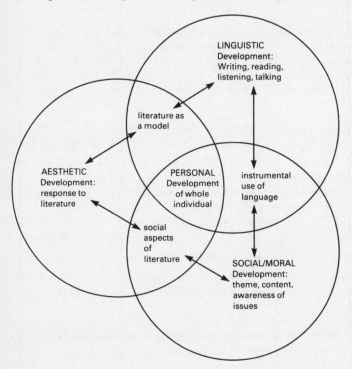

The territory over which teachers of English roam has been clearly and helpfully mapped in a recent report of the National Association for the Teaching of English's (NATE) Secondary Committee entitled *Best Laid Plans: English Teachers at Work.*[1] The model – reproduced in figure 1 – is presented as a 'picture of the possible interpretations of English as a subject'. It begs the question as to the actual experience 'enjoyed' by a sixteen-year-old near-school-leaver, who, through chance, has never moved out of one of those neat circles, locked into an unchanging scheme of things by the quirks of the department's staffing.

* See page 4 for an explanation of the asterisks on the next few pages.

'What's it all for anyway?'

Somehow an English department needs to clarify the stance it takes on the nature of the experience through which students will pass. The most recent HMI document *English From 5 to 16*, published by the DES in the autumn of 1984, fails to provide that clarification: it lays undue stress on objectives; it fails to grasp the fact that language awareness means more than knowing about grammar and, arguably, it reduces the significance of literature in the English programme. For many teachers of English, literature is indisputably at the centre of their work:

* Other practical uses of language are important and clearly children need to experience a wide variety of language use in different contexts from 11–18, but the gradual self-discovery of seeing themselves as active meaning makers through reading, writing and talking activities, prompted by the experience of powerful literature, represents ... an important, organising priority ... good literature is the most effective, precise, ordered form of language [and thus] it probably gives the best kind of preparation for mastering the practical uses of language.[2]

Ezra Pound argued that literature was a way of keeping words living and accurate; English teachers, too, are concerned with the emotional, imaginative and 'spiritual' development of the pupil. They are engaged in exploring and manipulating the blossoming interdependence of reading, talking, listening and writing:

* Reading, writing, talking about writing and talking in order to write must be continual possibilities: they overlap and interlock.[3]

The confidence in the modes of language which good teachers of English generate in their pupils enables them to 'know' the world and themselves more completely. Kafka commented:

* a book or a poem must be an ice-axe to break the sea frozen inside us.[4]

If you accept the fundamental truth beyond this startling image, it is clear that English is deeply concerned with the aesthetic, the creative and the spiritual.[5] Moreover, we are responsible for helping to develop within pupils the ability to participate sympathetically and constructively in society. This must involve an understanding of political, social and ethical issues and, most importantly, the ability to 'use' language with confidence – in order to learn, communicate and exploit life to its full.

Agonised debate on the lines of 'What's it all for anyway?' can all too easily lead to spilt coffee and heavy breathing at departmental meetings. It may help to focus on the issues by trying to establish an agreed order of priority for a set of quotations using a diamond formation; i.e. selecting one quotation as being the most significant for you (the two of you/the department), choosing two more that are important but clearly rank second – and so on, until you have negotiated a diamond-shaped collection of varied comments, as shown in figure 2.

Figure 2

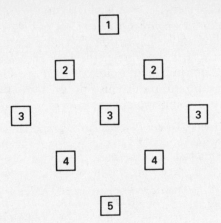

Through the preceding pages I have marked a number of quotations from a variety of sources with an asterisk. These, with those offered below, provide the basis for a valuable departmental discussion on the lines suggested above:

* 'Books? You should see our house,' said Andrew. 'We've got thousands.' 'We've got some books,' said Victor. 'Three or four . . . I read so slow I can't tell what's funny and what isn't.'[6]

* If talking and walking were taught in most schools we might end up with as many mutes and cripples as we have non-readers.[7]

* [English is] essentially to foster, improve and refine the individual's ability to use the mother-tongue – to use it fully, flexibly, effectively, sensitively, and to use it for all the varied purposes which one's native language must serve in a modern civilised community.[8]

* A linguistic approach to language may offer the best possibility of constructing a unifying framework for work in English.[9]

* English studies plainly have an important part to play in promoting the open society.[10]

Theory vs practice: classroom observation

Not only is it difficult to forge departmental certainty in terms of philosophy, but there is also the problem of matching high-flown theory against the reality of classroom practice. We say some strange things sometimes, both to children and about them.

- 'Miss X teaches the oral, free bit. I balance it with the formal work.'
- 'Before you get on with your assignment, I'll tell you a story as a reward.'
- 'Did you count the words? I did. In this poem there are 147 words.'
- 'You've got sloppy since you've been doing Literature.'
- 'Stop behaving like a couple of girls.'

A valuable focus for analysing the real nature of the English curriculum is to discuss the results of classroom observation – the observation either of a colleague or of oneself. Without this kind of knowledge, there can be no certainty as to the range of activities, the language use of teacher and chldren, the pace and timing of the work, the appropriateness of the material, or the sensitivity of the teacher to the needs of the individual child.

The teacher in the study included in figure 3[11] is in her second year of teaching and is learning to grapple with mixed ability grouping and a department who give her her head/allow her to make her own mistakes/do their own thing! She, at least, is clear in her own mind as to her intentions:

> I want to explore through reading, discussion and personal writing the subject of Ghost and Horror Stories. In particular, I want to find out what it is that attracts us to ghost stories . . . I want the children to produce a story of their own which, hopefully, avoids all the cliché'd traps usually associated with such stories.

How successful has she been?[12]

The teacher doesn't present herself, perhaps, in the best light, and it is not in any way a systematic piece of observation. Without hearing the children talk and sharing their writing it is not possible to be certain in judging the quality of the learning going on through those three weeks. Some questions do need facing, however:

- Is the time taken too long or too short?
- Has there been something of value for *all* the children in the class?
- Is there enough variety?
- How could the library problem have been solved?
- What went wrong on Fridays?
- Is the discussion work appropriately organised?

Figure 3   Notes on a programme of work: autumn term 1983

The teacher: Has just started her second year of teaching. Generally a good/sound probationary year; a few of the usual problems but thought by the department and the school to be a good bet for the future.

The class: A second-year mixed ability group. Number in class: 26.

THE TEACHER'S NOTES

Plan	Lesson	Comment
Lesson 1 (70 minutes) To start reading *'Mr. Corbett's Ghost'* by Leon Garfield. Then talk about the opening 2 chapters and discuss how mood and atmosphere are created by description – especially in Chapter 2.	**Week 1** Reading took shorter time than I thought it would. The 'discussion' was mainly 'me' telling 'them' to find certain words and passages and then asking them how these added to the pictures they have built up in their minds. In the end, we made a list of the 'describing' words in chapter 2!	Pupils enjoyed the reading but I wasn't happy with the discussion afterwards. As usual, it was me talking and leading and really only about 5 pupils contributed anything worthwhile. Not a bad lesson but could have been better!
Lesson 2 (70 minutes) To continue with idea of how an author uses words to build up mood and atmosphere. Read them a short story: *'The Austin 7'* by Anita Jackson and then, at the end, ask pupils to write down all the elements/words/phrases that contribute to 'Ghostliness' of the story.	Went straight into *'Austin 7'* story. Not a class set, therefore I read it to them and they listened. It's a good story with a pleasing twist at the end. They all seemed to enjoy it and then spent 15 minutes making their lists; we will go through these next time.	Very pleased! The list making idea, started last lesson with *'Mr. C's Ghost'* worked well and they all understood what I wanted them to do. Most of the success of the lesson should be attributed to *'The Austin 7'* story which is very good indeed!
Lesson 3 (35 minutes) Ask 3 or 4 pupils to read out their lists (based on *'The Austin 7'* story) and to use these as a 'lead in' to show them how the author adds the various ingredients of the story at different times to gain the final effect.	Last lesson on a Friday! They were very boisterous and rather silly. I thought they would enjoy this lesson because they had worked so well on their lists at the end of the previous lesson. We only got through 2 lists and had no real discussion — read chapter 3 of *'Mr. C's Ghost'* for the final 10 mins. of the lesson.	A pity they were in such a silly mood as I felt we were ready to make good progress today. Once again I thought the 'ground work' had been done but that the point of the lesson was never achieved. Disappointing!
Lesson 4 (70 minutes) To go back to the plan for lesson 3 and for them to think about how stories are put together — *'Austin 7'* and *'Mr. Corbett's Ghost'*. Read more of *'Mr. C's Ghost'*.	**Week 2** Much better today. Used the 'ingredients' idea and made a long list of the ingredients for the story on the board. Then talked about how these ingredients are put together — the recipe for the story. Most of them seemed to understand how the author used the ingredients to create the story. Continued reading of *'Mr. C's Ghost'*.	Very pleased with how the ingredients/recipe idea was received. They were much more sensible and calm today. Appeared to be interested and to be understanding the ideas involved in putting a story together. Enjoying the Garfield story also.

Plan	Lesson	Comment
Lesson 5 (70 minutes) To write up the work on *'The Austin 7'* story in their exercise books. To tell the story briefly in their own words and then to write down the lists of words and phrases. When finished to complete the reading of *'Mr. C's Ghost'*!	They worked quietly and sensibly on the written task but, as always with a M.– A. group, they worked at very different speeds. Some had finished after about 20 minutes, others had not finished by the end of the lesson. I had wanted to finish reading *'Mr. C's Ghost'* together but told the early finishers to carry on reading on their own.	Pleased with the level of concentration and the obvious hard work displayed as they got on with the writing. A pity the timing is never easy to organise as it was rather a 'messy' way to finish the reading of the story but it's the price one pays for M. — A. teaching groups!
Lesson 6 (35 minutes) Had arranged with the school librarian to make available as much fiction and non-fiction on Ghosts/Horror etc as possible. We (librarian and I) will then help pupils to choose a book for private reading	Friday again! Librarian saw me earlier that day to tell me she would not be there (meeting at County Library) but had put all the books out ready for me. I did not have a chance to go and check. Collected in exercise books (*all* had finished written work!) and tried to organise the giving out of the library books. Not helped by constant stream of pupils arriving from other lessons to "find a book about" etc. Just about managed to give every pupil a book but there was no choice involved.	A disaster! The books were OK but not very inspiring and the amount of 'private reading' was minimal. Will see librarian next week to organise another library lesson. Went home miserable again!
Lesson 7 (70 minutes) 2 aims:– (i) To get them started on writing their own stories and (ii) To sort out Friday's library disaster. If possible to have them in library for whole double lesson and to reorganise the reading books & start the writing.	**Week 3** Library was already booked for one of the lessons so I decided to concentrate upon getting them started on their own stories. Back to the ingredients idea! I talked for about 15 mins. and then they started to plan their stories by writing down the ingredients. i stressed that only after careful planning and notes in rough could they start copying up. Gave back exercise books. Told them to bring in library books for tomorrow's lesson.	Most of them worked very well. I went round and talked to individuals about their plans and ingredients and there are some pleasing ideas. Some (as usual!) rushed the planning and preparation to get on with the story but none had finished by the end of the lesson.
Lesson 8 (70 minutes) 'Booked' the library for the double lesson to give them an opportunity to change library books and continue with their stories. Some will probably finish their stories quite quickly and have a fair time for private reading.	Worked very well. It was a great help having the assistance of the librarian & by the end of the lesson all the pupils had got a suitable book to read. The writing is also going very well, some of the keen ones are writing pages! Set a homework to carry on with either the Story or private reading.	Very pleased. A great help having the books sorted out by the librarian — meant that I could give my time to the written work. The stories are coming on well and most should get them finished next lesson.
Lesson 9 (35 minutes) To finish off the stories and have them ready to hand in by the end of the lesson. Private reading of library books as they finish the writing.	Quite good (the best Friday lesson for several weeks!) Most finished their stories during the course of the lesson but the level of concentration on the reading by those who had finished was not very high. 4 pupils still had to finish and took their books home with them to finish over the weekend.	Will read the stories and mark/comment and then choose a few to read out to the class next week.

There are other questions too which you might wish the teacher to consider. Significantly, she knew things weren't right; a week or so afterwards she wrote:

> Thankfully, half term was at hand. I had reached that point where I suddenly found myself acutely at a loss for ideas to use in the classroom; many ideas seem so stereotyped and hackneyed.

This is the point where a policy of mutual support and collaboration within a department becomes invaluable. Without it, things fall apart.

> The resources that you share do involve planning, obviously; so a department, or members of it, have to get together. An atmosphere of openness and of saying what went well (or plummeted) is the result.[13]

The *reality* of classroom practice is what we must focus upon. In order to improve it we must observe it; share ideas, resources and approaches; and take heed of the perceptions about learning that children and teachers have.

The children first:

> From this lesson I've learnt that you've got to communicate if you want to get anywhere. It helps to work in groups, and problems are solved much more quickly.[14]
>
> I like it when we read each other's work, especially when it's stories or poems. We can usually tell what's good and bad about them.

Teachers, for their part, are only too well aware of the problems of matching theory to practice; articulating them, however, is scarcely half the battle.

Teachers' concerns: an agenda for action

A group of teachers was asked *to write down those aspects of children's literature that concerned them as individuals.* The responses provide a catalogue of anxiety, but also, perhaps, an agenda for action:

- We should try to abolish the distinction between 'school-approved reading' and 'own choice reading' since this is where élitism starts.

- Too often we expect children to *write* about what they read.

- There are insufficient books available with female characters.

- Do children have a chance to read at school in silence?

- There isn't enough variety.

- Do teachers share good books enough?

There are easily recognisable, but resilient, pressures: examinations, parents, lack of resources. We are anxious about the mismatch between the children's tastes in story and our own; about censorship, either of 'non-standard' English or of books that seem over-violent or sexually permissive; of systems of book purchase for libraries and English departments that seem random and, in consequence, prove to be irrelevant to the children's experience.

Moreover, outside the classroom, the world is changing faster than ever, both in terms of technology and in the social, political and economic demands made upon us all. Inevitably, the sharpest edge of change cuts the youngsters leaving school. The ripples wash back through the years of secondary schooling that hitherto had been becalmed: disillusioned attitudes to ill-fitting, pseudo-academic content and curriculum harden earlier and more certainly.

> Unlucky every [child] since the late seventies, launched into a world of unemployment. Class mobility . . . is at an end. And it has hit girls even worse than it has hit boys . . . No new generations of working class children can hope now even for a job, let alone a better job than their parents.[15]

On a good day, though, the changing world can be seen to offer an exciting challenge for teachers of English. There are opportunities to be exploited, worthwhile battles to be won and a generation of children for whom English offers the best hope in school for an education that is relevant, searching and deeply rooted in their needs, experience and natural hope.

The intention of this book is both to explore those aspects of English where change is most pressing and offers the greatest potential, and to provide guidance for English departments as to strategies, resources and priorities in these key areas of development. The book should provide agenda for discussion, programmes for action, food for thought and some ammunition for defending policy and attacking those who hinder progress – or ask stupid questions! We shall look at the significance of learning through Drama and its relationship with English; at media studies; at issues of race, gender and relevance in children's literature; at language policies and language awareness – and many other related issues.

Teachers in general, and teachers of English in particular, are all too readily misunderstood. Such misunderstanding usually heralds an even sadder failure to grasp the fact that education, above all, is for children. 'See here,' says the headmaster in the process of haranguing one of his English teachers in David Storey's novel *Saville*,

> 'it's my opinion you're a very good teacher . . . you're arrogant and rude, but that's your youth; a few years of what I've been through and you'll have those edges knocked off.'

Later, the head gives this shabby picture of what he sees as the purpose of education:

> 'After all . . . where are most of these children off to? When they leave here the majority'll go into factories that don't go down the pit; they'll work on the roads, they'll dig holes and clear out ditches; the girls'll do nought but work in a mill, get married and have children: children we'll be expected to do summat with . . . All thy wants to teach them is how to read a rent book, add up the week's wages and write a letter of application if they want a job'[16]

The mills have largely gone and the factories are closing down. But the world is closing in on such bleak, mean-minded views of education. Departments of English, have an enormous responsibility to defend what is unchangeable and, at the same time, accommodate to a world of rapid change. Only by collaboration, mutual support and trust, and an evolving certainty about priorities can the children's interests be secured. The curriculum we provide for them must offer balance, as well as excitement, variety and an awareness of the power and beauty of language.

Nobody is moving along the right lines. English should be fun – we had riotous fun in English. With enjoyment, it all clicks into place, sooner or later. You have to do the basics – we did a lot of formal work by stealth – but you should do them briefly, like brushing your teeth. And we push children into literary skills too fast.[1]

No doubt fired by The Great Debate and a remorseless passion for Basic Skills, the University of Salford ran, in April 1982, a two-day course for 'secondary school teachers confronted with problems in the teaching of English language'. The first day's programme was as follows:

9.00 – 9.30	Registration
9.30 – 10.45	Spelling
10.45 – 11.15	COFFEE
11.15 – 12.30	Vocabulary
12.30 – 1.30	LUNCH
1.30 – 2.45	Grammar and Punctuation
2.45 – 3.15	TEA
3.15 – 4.30	Comprehension

Such a stark programme seems a far cry from the English of 'personal growth' – apparently we had come a long way since the Dartmouth Seminar of 1965! One wonders, for example, at the use of upper case for the obviously highly significant meal breaks! It is, however, a sharp reminder of the extent to which 'English' can be distorted. Little sign on that day – it *was* 1 April – that language was something to savour, exploit and value; still less that the major task facing teachers of English is to create a learning environment where the pupils write, read, talk and listen with a growing sense of confidence. It is all too easy to forget this and to focus instead on a drab, utilitarian English which the children merely endure. The consequence is inevitable: at no point in the process of learning to read, for example, would it dawn upon these deprived children that reading is something that people do to add pleasure to their lives.

It needn't be so. The following boy's teacher has passed on the vital truth about the reading experience:

13th April 1984

Dear Ms Kemp,
   I thought your book 'Gowie Corby Plays Chicken' – Brilliant. I thought this because of the way it was wrote. I prefer books in which you can be the character . . . I thought it was clever how you made Gowie out to be a meanie and as the book goes on he turns into an angel. It was also very clever how at the end he still has a bit of the devil in him . . .

Damion Speight (Morley, Yorks.)[2]

Spreading the word: reading policy

Confidence in reading makes available to children a world that the insecure reader can never enjoy; it can unfold a network of experience, information and feeling. It provides a means by which we know the world and ourselves more completely.

Stumbling after meaning
It helps in planning for the development of children's reading to be aware of what it feels like to be an insecure reader, to grapple with text that threatens never to make sense. Bob Moy's English Centre publication *Readers and Texts: The Reading Process*[3] suggests one way of reminding ourselves of failure:

> For best effect work with a partner. One of you should read the first paragraph. The other should read the second. Try to note carefully *everything* that happens to each of you each time: the effects on your body, your mind, your personality, your performance, your self-image, your general behaviour.

Ereht saw llits on ngis fo eht srehto. Eht gninis dah deppots sa yeht dehcaorppa eht pmac. Won ereht saw enoon ot eb nees. Neht yeht was no eht pot fo eno fo eht sexob a taerg etihw god.

Ti saw on derbhguoroht. Tub ti dah kcuts ot sti tsop – ekilnu eht rehto step. Yeht dah deraeppasid nehw eht elbuort tsrif nageb. Won yeht erew no eht tops. Yeht erew deppart.

For both of you, as listener or reader, it is a salutary experience: as reader stumbling after meaning, or as listener impatiently fretting for the sentence to end. At what speed must you read before 'comprehension' can occur? When should the teacher intercede to prompt and guide? What do *you* do when an obstacle of a word looms ahead and the panic swells?

Sensitivity to the individual child's needs is fundamental, but an awareness of the kind of reading experience a school provides for its pupils is crucial too. Such an experience – all too likely to be a haphazard one – provides one measure by which children come to value the reading habit or perhaps, unhappily, to regard it thus: 'The majority of the class do not enjoy reading; it's not just that they find there are more attractive diversions, they positively resist it.'[4]

The pupil's perspective

Natalie and Dean are third-year pupils at an 11–18 comprehensive school. They were asked by their English teacher to record their reading activities in one week in all subjects; the results can be seen in figure 4.

Figure 4 Records of reading activities

NATALIE

Period →	1	2	3	4	5	6	7	8
Subject →	Drama	French	← P.E. →		History →		Music	Maths
MONDAY		READ QUESTIONS FROM BLACKBOARD				READ CHAPTER FROM TEXT BOOK 3 TIMES	READ ONE PIECE	READ QUESTIONS IN TEXT BOOK
	English →		Science →	← Games →			Maths	French
TUESDAY	READ 'THE OUTSIDERS' AS A CLASS		READ QUESTIONS ON WORK SHEET				READ QUESTIONS IN TEXT BOOK	READ QUESTIONS ON WORK SHEET
	Maths	English	Science		Geography	French	Religious Studies	
WEDNESDAY	READ QUESTIONS	READ WORDS OFF SHEET; DICTIONARY	READ QUESTIONS ON TEST PAPER		READ BLACKBOARD →		READ TEXT BOOK AND WORKSHEET	
	French	Maths	← Home Economics →				Geography →	
THURSDAY	READ FROM TEXT BOOK	READ FROM TEXT BOOK	READ COOKERY BOOK →					
	French	History	Chemistry		Maths	English	Home Economics	
FRIDAY	READ QUESTIONS ON ASSESSMENT PAPER →		READ WORKSHEET		READ QUESTIONS ON TEST BOOK	READ OWN BOOK ↓ (USSR)		

DEAN

	French	Religious St.	Maths		Geography		Physics	
MONDAY	READ QUESTIONS IN FRENCH	READ SHEET ON 'ISLAM'	READ THROUGH WORK DONE LAST WEEK AND QUESTIONS		READ SHEET AND BLACKBOARD		READ QUESTIONS ON WORKSHEET	
	History →		Drama	German	? →			
TUESDAY	READ ABOUT 'RACE TO THE POLE' SCOTT JUST LOSING TO AMUNDSEN			READ PAGE OF GERMAN	HOUSE RUGBY COMPETITION →			
	English →		Maths	German	Science		French	German
WEDNESDAY	FINISHED 'ACROSS THE BARRICADES' THEN READ 'OLIVER TWIST'		WE READ QUESTIONS	READ BLACKBOARD AND GERMAN BOOKS	READ QUESTIONS IN TEST		READ FRENCH CARTOON STRIP	READ QUESTION SHEET
	German	History	Engineering Drawing →				Biology →	
THURSDAY	READ GERMAN BOOK AND SHEETS	AS TUESDAY					READ WORKSHEET	
	German	PE	Maths	French	Music	English	Engineering Drawing	
FRIDAY	READ SHEET	WENT FOR AN E Y E TEST!			READ A BOOK ABOUT SYNTHESISERS	READ 'OLIVER TWIST' – PLAYSCRIPT		

NB SILENT READING IN TUTOR TIME

As with many investigations into the child's perceptions of school –
pupil pursuit, where an outside observer follows a pupil through his or
her lessons during a day or so, for example, can be particularly
illuminating – these pictures of a week's reading diet uncover some
interesting aspects of the school's dilemma in devising a coherent
reading policy. *Would you agree*:

- that there was not enough *sustained* reading? (Note, though, the one
  reference to USSR – *U*ninterrupted *S*ustained *S*ilent *R*eading;
  Natalie, Friday period 6.)

- that only rarely does the reading appear to provoke any *real* response?
  (But note Dean's unsolicited enthusiasm for the 'Race to the Pole';
  Tuesday 1 and 2.)

- there is too much emphasis on worksheet and questioning?

There is a suggestion too that Natalie and Dean's teachers are failing
to consider their needs as *individual* readers. There is no indication that
the maxim 'give the right book to the right child at the right time' is
being followed. (One primary school child caught the point precisely in a
troubled aside to an HMI: 'This book tells me more than I really want to
know about elephants'!) Only by closely monitoring children's individual
reading habits and attitudes can we be sure that books retain
significance for them as they move through secondary school. It is not
just a question of them shedding the label of 'reluctant reader', it is
concerned with making reading part of their lives, both now and as they
grow older.

One group of teachers, from both primary and secondary schools,
'brainstormed' on those factors that favour reading development:

- Wanting to.
- Writing.
- Listening and talking.
- Encouragement.
- Example
- Being read to.
- Sharing.
- Necessity.
- Parents.
- Inspiration.
- Imitation

The school – and, above all, the English department – clearly can greatly influence the patterns of, and attitudes to, reading prevalent amongst the children.[5] The department needs to make explicit through its reading policy the answers to such questions as:[6]

- Is the central library widely used?
- Is there a class library system?
- Are the functions of both, if they exist, clearly defined and understood by children and staff?
- How are books recommended to children?
- Is there a school bookshop?
- Are books displayed?
- Can the children read for pleasure or must they always write a review?
- Do the teachers read outside school?
- Are the teachers seen reading *in* school?
- Does the school make use of the 'Writers in Schools' scheme?
- Can children take books home?
- Are parents involved?
- Are there opportunities to share responses to books?
- Are the relationships between pupils and teacher and pupil and pupil mutually supportive?
- Is a varied reading diet being offered: story; poem; novel; play; children's own writing?

Above all, perhaps, it is the choice of text and the strategies the teacher adopts for sharing and exploring it with child, group or class that are most important. Taking the only set of thirty class readers from the back of the book cupboard, blowing away the dust and settling for a leisurely read around the class, with occasional interruptions for dutiful comprehension exercises, is a certain recipe for tedium:

[Is it] reasonable to expect young readers to work alone to get meaning from texts, answering in writing written questions set in advance by an unknown adult and marked later in the reader's absence by a teacher, one of whose prime concerns in assessing the response will be to receive a fully-formed reply, properly constructed, properly punctuated and spelled, and neatly handwritten against the clock[?][7]

Choice of text: what criteria; whose choice?

Why is it that adults are taking such a great interest in children's literature? Adults read about the traumas of divorce, constant bullying and the worries of sex in *The Secret Diary of Adrian Mole Aged 13¾* by Sue Townsend. Wasn't that a best seller? Nobody worried about children reading that. On the back cover, Tom Sharpe commented, 'Here is a book to touch the hearts of three generations.' Doesn't that include children?

Before the BRILLIANT Judy Blume, there wasn't a writer discussing the true facts of life, so kids were satisfied with Enid Blyton's books of adventure and fantasy with a strong plot. But now we have been blessed with Ms Blume, we are enjoying reading more. For instance a Famous Five book usually only gets read about twice in a lifetime by any one person, but only yesterday I completed reading my set of eleven Judy Blume books for about the seventh time.

Naomi Watkins (aged 12½) Warley, West Midlands, in a letter to the *Guardian*, August 1984[8]

The criteria for choosing books differ markedly from person to person; this is especially true of children and teachers. One survey[9] suggested the following 'other influences' on choice:

On teachers' choice of children's books:

- Price.
- Availability.
- Written by a well-known author.
- Published by a well-known publisher.
- Recommended by a friend.
- Has been on TV.
- Socially or politically significant.
- 'I enjoyed it myself as a child.'
- It is part of a cultural heritage.
- It is innovative.

On the other hand, the children's choice:

- Has been on TV.
- Has been a film.
- Has been 'advertised'.
- Has been recommended by a friend or teacher.
- Is by a well-tried author.

- Is one of a series, has known characters.
- Price.

Given the mismatch between the two sets of criteria, it is important to devise a system for choosing fiction that respects the children's instinctive preferences, but allows their prejudice (and ours!) to be questioned and, above all, for new doors to open for them. The teacher's influence can be profound. One list of 'most popular authors' drawn up by fourth-year juniors in an urban primary school indicates how influential the well-read, book-loving adult can be: Bernard Ashley, Roald Dahl, C. S. Lewis, Gene Kemp, Ian Serraillier, Leon Garfield, Margaret Mahy, Alison Prince.

Case study: a school's fiction policy

The Head of Department, David Parmiter, has reservations about the use of the class reader, but in the two years since his appointment all his attempts to move away from it have proved fruitless. Most of the department insist on sharing a class reader with all classes, including the mixed ability groups in the lower school. Recommended texts in year three include, for example, *The Machine Gunners* (Robert Westall), *Fireweed* (Jill Paton Walsh), and Steinbeck's *The Red Pony*. Each classroom has two tightly packed shelves of books which are available for loan to the children, but there are only three such classrooms regularly used by the department. English is therefore taught in a variety of strange environments, including, on one occasion, a science lab. To compensate for this, a number of book boxes have been collected and are available to staff, though the number of boxes (six) and the number of books in each (thirty) are insufficient.

David follows a conscious policy of purchasing paperbacks, arguing that the children are more attracted to them. After a series of contentious departmental meetings, he has begun to 'grade' the books according to their perceived difficulty, and the department's extensive lists of recommended books includes that information. Both the school library and the school bookshop (run by the fourth year and with the accounts done by the lower sixth Economics group!) are significant adjuncts to the department's fiction policy. Most of the department encourage detailed book reviews from the children, though David is experimenting in the lower school with an easily completed report sheet which involves the children in noting down, in one line, the simplest information:

Date	Title/Author of book	Source (home, library . . .)	Pages read	Times read	Comment

The department's filing cabinet has a drawer full of 'comprehension passages', many of them relating to class readers. Recently, the department organised a Book Week which included a film (*Lord of the Flies*), a visiting writer who spoke to 350 children in the school hall, a competition to design publicity posters for the school bookshop, and a large display of new fiction provided by the Education Library Service.

David Parmiter defends his policy with vigour, but admits to three areas of doubt:

1 The over-reliance on class readers, some of which are a trial for all concerned.
2 The disappointing pass rate at O level in Literature and the resulting small groups studying English at A level.
3 The decline in interest in books in the third year and above.

Where is he going wrong?

Sharing text: involvement and response

> Make up a poem which shows one or more examples of ordinary, masculine, feminine, and triple rhyme, assonance and consonance. It must also show examples of the use of similies [sic], metaphors, symbolism, onomatopoeia, imagery, irony – and a pun if possible. Give the metre of your poem some thought and comment on the mood and tone of your poem . . . This will be difficult [etc.].[10]

Although this example is surely an invention of the contributor to *NATE News*, from where it was taken, there is enough truth in it to make us feel uncomfortable. We cannot expect children to be moved by what they read if the tasks they are forced to do touch only their capacity for boredom: a lingering death by fatuous worksheet!

Examinations don't help – although it is increasingly possible to avoid the worst constraints.[11] Can we expect, as one board did recently, CSE candidates to cope with the complexities of Anthony Thwaite's poem 'Looking On' in the sombre isolation of an examination hall, staring alternately at the fidgeting back of the candidate in front and the stark questions designed to 'test understanding'?

> 1 Anthony Thwaite has focused his main messages on the last two lines of each verse of this poem. What do you understand of each of the two-line portions at the end of the verses?
>
> (6 marks)
>
> 2 Write briefly about the ideas contained in this poem. Are these realistic comments to make?
>
> (4 marks)[12]

Small wonder that poetry for many children is something you 'do' in school and not outside, or indeed after it. It needs to be shared, not dredged for meaning; to be part of the structure upon which 'English' rests, not a frill that embarrasses the teacher and alienates the children. Two quotations to act as a warning:

> There's only one poetry anthology in the school – and I don't know where *it* is [from a probationary teacher (1984)].

> If I was given the choice never to do poetry again, I would not do it. In my whole life, reading poetry, never have I enjoyed it. I would arrange separate classes for children who wanted to do it [from a fourth-year pupil and, significantly perhaps, one who was doing O level].[13]

Sharing poetry with children highlights the teacher's difficulty in devising strategies for engaging children in what they read. Being confident in handling poetry in the classroom presupposes three things: certainty of purpose (knowing *why* you want to share a particular poem); certainty of material (knowing what works in the classroom); and possessing a range of techniques going beyond what Peter Benton has called the 'three box syndrome' – you read it; you discuss it; they write about it. Appendix 4 provides a list of poems that 'work'.

It is not enough for an English department to put a limp reference to poetry in its guidelines. 'Wherever possible, poetry should be encouraged.' – HMI John Taylor has castigated such shillyshallying:

> 'Poetry is the excess baggage that you ditch when the going gets tough.'
> On the contrary, it should be at the centre of what we do.

It is the *quality* of language that is the reason for this, the power and savour of words. Without that richness of language experience, what hope is there for an articulate and sensitive human race?

Case study: an experiment in poem making
The teacher: Mick Connell, Head of English at St Bernard's RC Comprehensive School, Rotherham. The poem: 'The Grauballe Man' by Seamus Heaney, in *North*, Faber (1975). Peter Abbs's book *English Within the Arts* (pp. 72–3) is the inspiration for this work:

> I claim no originality for the ideas offered here but present this brief account of some exciting and demanding classroom practice.
> I sought a method by which to introduce a fourth-year O level Literature group to that inner world of feeling that finds expression in poetry; a method that would prove intense, challenging and memorable for them. I believe that the writing session described below offered my pupils this chance to grapple with the rigours of art-expression and to experience the satisfaction of crafting their own poem.
> We had an hour and twenty minutes available. Privately I considered allowing them time to redraft their poems later, if they wished, but initially I told them whatever they wrote should be 'completed' in that session.
> I had brought two photographs of the Grauballe man after excavation. One showed him full-length within his peat bed, the other was a haunting

close-up of a delicately half-closed hand. I told the pupils nothing about the photographs.

Two of the pupils were asked to write down what they remembered of that lesson's structure. This is how they described it:

'1   We looked at the photographs for 5 minutes. We jotted down, at random, words, ideas and images that occurred to us.

2   We gathered together and talked about the photographs and what we thought of them. Up to this point our teacher had told us nothing about them at all! (10 minutes)

3   We went away and tried to find some connecting ideas and images in our original jottings. We also added any new ideas at this stage. (15 minutes)

4   We formed small groups and chatted together briefly about what we were trying to write. We didn't talk much though because we wanted to finish them. (10 minutes)

5   We had 40 minutes in which to "craft" our ideas into a finished piece. We nearly all needed longer and we sat through break to finish them off.'

Cath W. and Steven B.

The success of the session and the power of the writing that emerged left me with that rare flush of teacher-excitement. Two aspects seemed particularly valuable:

1   The pupils had experienced an insight into the creative and crafting process of art-expression. In contrast with so much classroom writing which can become an empty ritual, this session had exhausted and exhilarated them.

2   Each pupil had been uniquely 'prepared' for Heaney's poem. The writing task had brought them into close focus with the text, narrowing and deepening their involvement with the poem. (Incidentally, Heaney himself wrote his poem in response to the very same photographs.)

Further writing workshops are planned. I have photographs assembled for an identical session on Larkin's 'An Arundel Tomb'[14] and I hope also to extend it to the use of personal and historical artefacts with George Macbeth's 'The Drawer'.[15]

Steven B's final draft:

How long has he laid there?
This anonymous man of centuries past.
How long has the peat been his life-taker . . . his coffin
Yet, in death, his preserving mantle?

His body, blackened by the peat, seems to cry out for help.
His arms, his pelvis . . . twisted, like a coiled snake,
seem to be trying to disassociate themselves,
take on a life of their own.

His body, though, is muscular,
Well-veined, like roads on a map.
Veins, like fat snakes,
run through his body like streams.

His head is laid to one side,
as though resting on a stone.
The veins of his twisted neck,
Sticking out like the rearing head of a monster.

His skin, like a sheet, clothes him,
so thin, flaky, crisp as a snowflake.
His bones, decayed, yellow,
now rooted into the peat.

How long had he laid there?
In the moist peat, the dungeons of death,
before his body was discovered
and again laid to rest.

DARTS: Directed Activities Related to Texts

While poetry is perhaps most vulnerable to insensitive handling in the classroom, fiction can be similarly subjected to a drab regimen of extract and question. The consequence of this is a dawning misunderstanding by children as to the purpose of reading. There are, of course, other ways of approaching the problem: see, for example, '36 Things to do with a Poem' by Geoff Fox and Brian Merrick and '24 Things to do with a Book' by Geoff Fox.[16] Moreover, since the publication of *The Effective Use of reading*,[17] there has been a growing interest in 'DARTS' techniques, or sometimes a sense of reassurance that tried approaches have received Schools Council approval! The publication of *Learning from the Written Word* has significantly carried this work forward.

The department could usefully discuss the extent to which individual members have used the techniques summarised in figure 5 and, in particular, to focus on the practicalities:

- What size groups?

- What kinds of text?

- What kind of talk occurs in the groups?

- What strategies 'work' best?

- When is a particular strategy appropriate?

- What are the benefits?

Figure 5 DARTS – Directed Activities Related to Texts

* All activities in small groups . . .

DELETION	QUESTIONS	SEQUENCING
CLOZE → (ii) **VARIATIONS** → (a) Delete longer chunks (b) Compare versions with other groups and the original. Children discuss the most appropriate word to fit a gap left in the text, either a random gap or, say, every 6th word. The word(s) negotiated should make sense, be 'grammatical', and fit in terms of style	(i) **OPEN** rather than closed. Open questions e.g. Why choose this title? What has the writer left out? demand thought, provoke argument and alter traditional views as to the relationship between reader and text. (ii) *PUPILS' QUESTIONS:* In pairs or threes, the children devise questions on the text (perhaps in role).	In small groups, the children are given a prose extract or poem cut into lines, segments or even individual words. By careful reading — and rereading — the group decides on an acceptable order. * THIS STRATEGY WORKS PARTICULARLY WELL WITH VERSE.

PREDICTION	ANALYSING TEXT	VISUAL REPRESENTATIONS OF TEXT
The children, from their knowledge of a text, predict what is going to happen next. * This works well as a whole class activity with the teacher releasing text line by line, or section by section, using an OHP.	The children are asked to: underline ↑ label or 'segment' text, for a specific purpose determined, probably, by the teacher. ('Segmenting': – isolating units of information – labelling of segments of text *without* teacher-provided labels.)	After reading the text, the children may draw maps, diagrams or complete tables — after due discussion!

- How do 'DARTS' fit into the overall policy for reading within the department?

Arguably, DARTS work best:

- in smaller groups (two or three);

- when the activity fits into a broader context, i.e. the text isn't chosen at random;

- when the children understand that their response is not 'right' or 'wrong';

- When the texts fit the strategy and both fit the group;

- when the strategy remains secondary to the text.

(Figure 5 does *not* include *all* the possible DARTS techniques, only those which seem particularly appropriate.)

TWO EXAMPLES

Example 1. Ho Thien's poem 'Green Beret' demonstrates some interesting aspects of using DARTS – in this case as a sequencing activity:

Green Beret

Ho Thien of the 4th Plains Unit wrote this down sixty days after New Year, after hearing the story from a woman of Dalat on the High Plateau.

> He was twelve years old,
> and I do not know his name.
> The mercenaries took him and his father,
> whose name I do not know,
> one morning upon the High Plateau.
> Green Beret looked down on the frail boy
> with the eyes of a hurt animal and thought,
> a good fright will make him talk.
> He commanded, and the father was taken away
> behind the forest's green wall.
> 'Right kid tell us where they are,
> tell us where or your father – dead.'
> With eyes now bright and filled with terror
> the slight boy said nothing.
> 'You've got one minute left kid,' said Green Beret,
> 'tell us where or we kill father,'
> and thrust his wrist watch against a face all eyes,
> the second hand turning, jerking on its way.
> 'OK boy ten seconds to tell us where they are.'
> In the last instant the silver hand shattered the sky
> and the forest of trees.

'Kill the old guy,' roared Green Beret
and shots hammered out
behind the forest's green wall
and sky and trees and soldiers stood
in silence, and the boy cried out.
Green Beret stood
in silence, as the boy crouched down
and shook with tears,
as children do when their father dies.
'Christ,' said one mercenary to Green Beret,
'he didn't know a damn thing
we killed the old guy for nothing.'
So they all went away,
Green Beret and his mercenaries.

The poem, however, is not complete. The children are given the remaining ten lines in a random order;

like tigers
protected by frail tears
across the High Plateau.
and in the moment that he cried out
And the boy knew everything,
far stronger than any wall of steel,
the trails the hidden places and the names,
they passed everywhere
He knew everything about them, the caves,
in that same instant,

The activity is absorbing in itself; it necessitates reading and re-reading the poem;[18] it raises interesting questions – about the way the poet 'builds on' what has gone before. Teachers who 'do' the activity in an in-service context usually argue about the punctuation.

All of which ignores the crucial fact that the poem 'works' – it moves to anger, it uplifts – when it is simply read aloud with no tricks.

Example 2. Prediction: a first-year group were asked to predict what was going to happen next in a short story they had read about a small boy called Charles. The teacher had left them alone (in the stock cupboard) with a cassette recorder:

Teacher:	You've all got to come to a decision as a group about what is going to happen next . . .
Gary:	Yes.
Heather:	Yeah, right then. (*Teacher leaves.*)
John:	Our decision is . . . (*Laughter.*)
Karen:	Let's think.

Gary:	I think . . .
	(*Heated and confused discussion.*)
Gary:	Listen. We're getting off the point. We've got to think what happens next.
John:	He goes to school the next day and something gets damaged . . .
Gary:	. . . that's valuable . . .
John:	He comes home and he says, 'Oh dad . . . somebody's broke . . .'
Gary:	And his father says, 'It wasn't you, was it?' Or something like that . . .
John:	And he says, 'No. It was Charlie' . . .
Heather:	(*In an affected tone*) Charles. Charles is a very naughty boy then.
John:	Yes. And then round comes the teacher . . .
Gary:	With a bill . . .
John:	Knock, knock.
	(*Laughter.*)
All:	Who's there?
Gary:	It's the teacher of your little naughty son. (*Laughter.*)
Heather:	It's broke . . .
John:	And this is the bill please sir.
Gary:	And his father says, 'Broken? Well I thought Charles did that. Charles . . .'
John:	'Who's he?'
Gary:	'Who's Charles?' Something like that. And he says, 'Son . . .'
Karen:	'He's the one who's been naughty.'
Gary:	'OK. I'll send the bill on to the school. Goodbye.'

The tape itself is difficult to transcribe because of the energy and enthusiasm of the group. Most interestingly, they are excited enough to slip into role play towards the end, re-enacting what they think happened in the story. But the tape raises other questions too, not least about the composition of groups: Karen and Heather are almost lost behind Gary and Kevin's boisterous involvement. One can only guess what they learned from the experience.

The writing process

The novelist J. L. Carr in *How Steeple Sinderby Wanderers Won the FA Cup*[19] presents an idiosyncratic picture of learning:

Children need only to be taught How to Learn, and to remember what they learnt for only as long as the remembrance was of any earthly use. So each Steeple Sinderby child spent 7½ hours each week learning Exact Observation, Speed Reading, Knowledge Retention and the Bright Ones got an important Extra – How to let Waffle wash over them whilst improving the time by thinking constructively.

As we know, children learn by making meaning through language, through the reading, writing, talking and listening they are engaged in, both in school and out of it. The overlap between these modes of language is continuous and the learning is most effective when the children are most actively engaged. For many children, writing is that aspect of language which yields the least reward and the most potential for failure, while for teachers it can become the means through which children are assessed, rather than the opportunity to extend horizons.

Learning through writing

> Most theories of literary analysis are . . . concerned with the relationship between the writer and the text, and the text and the audience, whilst in children's writing we need to look for what the writing does for the writer.[20]

Carolyn Steadman's analysis of children's writing in *The Tidy House*, from which the above quotation is drawn, is focused on three working-class girls aged between eight and nine. Her fundamental assertion that children's writing *is for the writer* as much as for the reader holds true in secondary schools as well:

> *Teacher:*   OK . . . when you sit down, pen in hand at home, who do you write it for?
>
> *Fourth–year*
> *Pupil:*   For yourself really, when you start thinking about it. When you start getting into things your own way, thinking in your own way. Like you said, it helps you to remember.

This pupil is talking about learning through writing in History, but English teachers need to recognise the power of writing, as well as its dangers; to ensure that the children write from experience, for themselves and for a variety of different audiences, and in as many different contexts and registers as possible. One alarming moment in the HMI report *Aspects of Secondary Education*[21] was the fifth-year O level Literature student who had just completed a 23,000 word summary of a Hardy novel – and was about to embark upon *Great Expectations*! It is a useful and illuminating exercise for a department to conduct a survey into the writing 'tasks' set to each class on a typical teaching day. One department produced a list of twenty-two different writing exercises, which has been summarised and categorised in figure 6.

Redrafting: 'manicuring the corpse'?

> We have all heard the groan in the classrooms, 'Do I have to copy it over?' This is the popular understanding of revision. Put a good manicure on the corpse.[22]

Figure 6 Twenty-two possible writing exercises

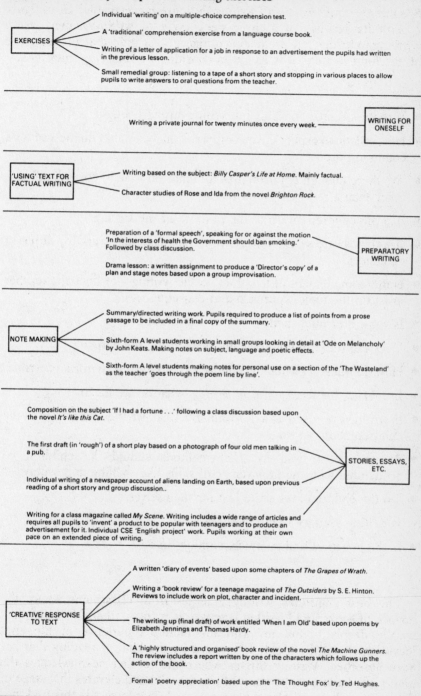

EXERCISES
- Individual 'writing' on a multiple-choice comprehension test.
- A 'traditional' comprehension exercise from a language course book.
- Writing of a letter of application for a job in response to an advertisement the pupils had written in the previous lesson.
- Small remedial group: listening to a tape of a short story and stopping in various places to allow pupils to write answers to oral questions from the teacher.

Writing a private journal for twenty minutes once every week. — WRITING FOR ONESELF

'USING' TEXT FOR FACTUAL WRITING
- Writing based on the subject: *Billy Casper's Life at Home*. Mainly factual.
- Character studies of Rose and Ida from the novel *Brighton Rock*.

PREPARATORY WRITING
- Preparation of a 'formal speech', speaking for or against the motion 'In the interests of health the Government should ban smoking.' Followed by class discussion.
- Drama lesson: a written assignment to produce a 'Director's copy' of a plan and stage notes based upon a group improvisation.

NOTE MAKING
- Summary/directed writing work. Pupils required to produce a list of points from a prose passage to be included in a final copy of the summary.
- Sixth-form A level students working in small groups looking in detail at 'Ode on Melancholy' by John Keats. Making notes on subject, language and poetic effects.
- Sixth-form A level students making notes for personal use on a section of the 'The Wasteland' as the teacher 'goes through the poem line by line'.

STORIES, ESSAYS, ETC.
- Composition on the subject 'If I had a fortune . . .' following a class discussion based upon the novel *It's like this Cat*.
- The first draft (in 'rough') of a short play based on a photograph of four old men talking in a pub.
- Individual writing of a newspaper account of aliens landing on Earth, based upon previous reading of a short story and group discussion..
- Writing for a class magazine called *My Scene*. Writing includes a wide range of articles and requires all pupils to 'invent' a product to be popular with teenagers and to produce an advertisement for it. Individual CSE 'English project' work. Pupils working at their own pace on an extended piece of writing.

'CREATIVE' RESPONSE TO TEXT
- A written 'diary of events' based upon some chapters of *The Grapes of Wrath*.
- Writing a 'book review' for a teenage magazine of *The Outsiders* by S. E. Hinton. Reviews to include work on plot, character and incident.
- The writing up (final draft) of work entitled 'When I am Old' based upon poems by Elizabeth Jennings and Thomas Hardy.
- A 'highly structured and organised' book review of the novel *The Machine Gunners*. The review includes a report written by one of the characters which follows up the action of the book.
- Formal 'poetry appreciation' based upon the 'The Thought Fox' by Ted Hughes.

How do you *know* when strategies for developing writing are working? Are the *range* and *balance* of writing in figure 6 acceptable? Does figure 7, with its account of a three-week cycle of writing activity, leave anything to be desired? In looking at figure 7, or indeed at any sequence of 'teaching writing', it is useful to consider the following questions:

* Was the original stimulus for writing strong enough?
* Is it realistic to expect the class to write on a common theme and for a common purpose?
* Are there enough opportunities for children to write for an audience other than a red-pen-toting teacher?
* Are the children aware of the purpose of the writing?
* Are they aware of the difference in language necessary for different audiences?
* Is there an element of 'contract' in the writing – or does the teacher insist on the topic, approach and consequences?
* Is work ever published?
* Does the redrafting go beyond 'manicuring the corpse'?
* How do you react when the children ask, 'How much must we write'?
* In looking for *development in writing*, what do we mean?
* Is writing ever used as a punishment? If so, what does that say to the children about writing?
* At what point and by what methods should the children be acquainted with the importance of skills like spelling and syntax?
* Do the children ever write just for themselves?
* Is writing seen as a craft? Do *you* write?
* Is the *process* valued as much as the *product*?

The best children's writing emerges from classrooms where the nuance of spoken and written language is recognised and fostered; it is usually deeply bound up with the child's experience of life and, inevitably, it will be highly influenced by the kind of reading that has been absorbed. Writing thrives where the teacher acknowledges the power of 'shaping at the point of utterance'[23] and elevates that stage of the process above all else. One teacher who understands this told me:

Figure 7 A three-week cycle of writing activity

CLASS: *1st year*
11–12 year olds

	PLAN	THE LESSON: WHAT ACTUALLY HAPPENED . . .
WEEK 1 **LESSON 1** 35 minutes Monday p.7	My overall intention is to develop the children's ability to write, both with greater clarity and a heightened awareness of the short story form. To establish a common starting point, I shall read 2 poems about relationships between adults and children: 'My Dad, Your Dad' by Kit Wright and 'The Identification' by Roger McGough. In groups, we shall discuss the poems and, in particular, list the qualities a good parent should have (!)	In fact, we spent far longer talking as a class about 'The Identification'. This class don't seem used to working in groups and the room we're forced into using is not ideal! Rightly or wrongly, we argued long and hard about what would happen after the poem ended: how the father would cope with his son's death.
LESSON 2 70 minutes Wednesday p. 1 + 2	(1) Read 'The Breadwinner' by Leslie Halward, a short story about a young boy's brave refusal to hand over his first week's pay packet to his drunken father. (2) Get groups to devise questions on points that interest them. (3) Discuss as a class possible areas for extended writing'. (4) Get kids writing in last 25 minutes.	It seemed like a good idea at the time: in fact I read the whole story except for the final paragraph or so — which I asked them to predict. We talked about this: I questioned non-committally, they theorised enthusiastically and then in pairs, wrote a brief conclusion to the story. It worked well, *but* it threw the timings wildly out. In the event, they were just about to start writing when the bell went. No time to set homework!
LESSON 3 70 minutes Friday 1 + 2	Period 1: Library lesson as usual Period 2: Reveal to the class 4 ideas *I've* had for a story. Discuss with class which one they think I should choose for further development. Then 'brainstorm' — random thoughts and phrases on the board. Ask children to suggest *their* 3 or 4 topics and then choose 1. Brainstorm. I start to write for 5 minutes — and the children too! Check on non-starters etc.	Wisely, I think, I cut the library period short – just gave them the chance to change books. No one liked my suggested short story themes, though there was more interest when I told them (briefly) a true story about an occasion when I ran away from home (as a child!). They were very good at suggesting areas for development for themselves — jealousy with brothers/sisters — Death in the Family — Parents who don't understand etc. Most of the children began writing with me, though I felt uncomfortable opting out after 5 minutes in order to check how things were going. On reflection, I gave them a reading homework because I wanted to keep close tabs on the early stages of the writing.

Continued on page 30

Figure 7 Continued from page 29

	PLAN	THE LESSON: WHAT ACTUALLY HAPPENED...
WEEK 2 **LESSON 4** 35 minutes Monday	Discuss variety of forms of writing with class; ensure that each child knows precisely where they are going with their story.	We looked at a range of possible ways of communicating a story: use of dialogue, pictures, description, character, reportage, letters etc. Each child wrote on a scrap of paper exactly what they intended to write and handed them in. A contract established! I wish I'd let them discuss their final choice with each other, but the bell went too soon.
LESSON 5 70 minutes Wednesday	Introduce the idea of clarity and economy – verbally first by getting them to instruct a volunteer to tie someone else's tie! Then in groups, write explicit instructions to a stranger trying to find the Sports Hall. Then give them the opening and concluding lines to a story and insist that their concluded version be less than 150 words!	Didn't work as well as I'd hoped: was my timing wrong? Some kids arrived late (from the head!) and they missed the point entirely. The short story idea (which I've used before) didn't work at all. Has the other story gone cold?
LESSON 6 70 minutes Friday	Library and 'Main' short story writing. First drafts to be finished by Monday. **Set Homework!**	A good lesson: nice 'workshop' atmosphere throughout. Everyone engaged at their own speed.
WEEK 3 **LESSON 7** 35 minutes Monday	Small groups (of 3) to discuss each other's first drafts.	A lot of heated discussion. Should I have provided a focus? There was certainly more criticism than positive response! I asked them to begin work on a second draft in the light of the comment from their friends.

LESSON 8
70 minutes
Wednesday
	Read 'Indian Camp' by Ernest Hemingway. Explain that all their stories will be 'published' and eventually put in the school library; in addition, each story will be sent to an individual, named child in the Primary School.	We enjoyed the break of sharing the story, not least, I suspect, because it was clearly read for its own sake: no worksheet! The publishing idea went down well: I got the timing right for once. Discussion centred on
		   — covers
		   — printing or handwriting
		   — which children would read it
		   — what kind of language would be appropriate for the child.
		
		3rd drafts begun.

LESSON 9 70 minutes Friday	Optional library lesson. Prepare stories for publication.	*Now*, the children's attention has come to focus on the surface skills of spelling, layout etc. On Wednesday next, we shall visit the top class in the Juniors and arrange for the readings to happen! I do wonder if I've rushed them too much . . . Should the children, for example, choose which story to publish from a range of attempts?

What do you do when you spill coffee over a pile of CSE coursework? The ink began to run and at least ten of the scripts were rapidly becoming illegible. I couldn't hand them back like that, could I? So I typed them out. The kids thought I was crazy at first; then one of them said, 'It's just like *real* writing isn't it, sir?' The typewriter became part of the classroom's equipment after that.

Talk

'I feel that I don't allow children to talk enough in both formal and informal ways . . . I feel constrained to produce something in writing.' This anonymous teacher works in a primary school where, many observers would suggest, the prevailing atmosphere is such that the work is invariably organised in groups and the children's talk is always nurtured and valued. For years secondary schools have been criticised for their inability to break the infamous 'rule of two thirds':[24] in the average classroom two thirds of every lesson is made up of talk, and two thirds of the talk comes from the teacher (which seems a modest estimate).

Despite the impact the cassette recorder has had, as well as the broad acceptance of the crucial role talk plays in learning, it is still true to say that 'Talking and listening by pupils are . . . not fully enough exploited.'[25] We nod approvingly when 'talk' is declared to be a 'good thing', but we have failed, for the most part, to ensure that our classrooms are places where children learn to talk and listen to each other without constraints shackling them; the teacher does not need to dominate. What the teacher does need to do is structure the work so that what is talked about deserves attention and builds on what has gone before. Moreover, the teacher has a responsibility to enable the children to learn the rules of a different game: not a 'rule of two thirds' but a 'rule of trust', where the children's right to learn actively rather than passively is guaranteed.

More than lip service?

'Quiet there. This is a language lesson so there should be no talking AT ALL.'

Charlie Lewis Plays For Time by Gene Kemp [26]

How would you compare your own department's (unspoken?) policy for talk with this drafted recently in an 11–18 comprehensive school?

What sort of talk?

The children should be able to/have the opportunity to:

- Ask relevant questions.
- Tell a story.
- Persuade someone.
- Chat.
- Speculate.
- Debate (formally and informally).
- Think aloud.
- Negotiate.
- Give instructions.
- Complain.
- Argue (and win).
- Argue (and lose graciously).
- Express or disguise feelings.
- Reach judgements.
- Summarise and arrive at a point of decision.

What strategies?

In the classroom

- DARTS techniques.
- Role play, leading to Drama.
- Brainstorming.
- Use of photos.
- Use of film, TV.
- Open-ended questioning.
- Ranking (putting things in an agreed/negotiated order).
- Pose *real* problems.
- Value the kids' contributions – don't disregard the anecdote.

In the department

- Tape-record lessons.
- Tape-record groupwork.
- Bear group dynamics in mind when drawing up class lists.
- Classroom furniture and geography should encourage group talk.
- Look at the other departments in the school; talk to them about talk.

Perhaps the most important element here is the extent to which the teacher can create a world in which the children feel free to take risks and where they believe without question in the significance of what they are doing. In the extract below, the children are deeply engaged in a role play where a mysterious house is being sold; by this stage of the transcript, everyone in the room (significantly cleared of desks) believes in what is happening:

Darren: What was it like at night when you were in bed?

Simon: Well, it was a bit creepy. (*Pause.*)

Lucy: Did you hear any noises in the loft?

Simon: No, only really rats.

(*Pause.*)

John: Do the radiators make noises?

Simon:	Not all the time.
Gill:	Do the stairs really creak?
Simon:	No.
Wayne:	Had you actually heard any screaming or anything?
Simon:	Only next-door neighbours.
Wayne:	Can you hear the thermostat at night when the water's warming up?
Simon:	No ...
Lucy:	Do the floorboards squeak at night?
Simon:	No.
Wanda:	Was there sort of noises from under the floorboards? As if someone was under them?
Simon:	No ...
Carla:	Did you hear things that go bump in the night?

It reads and sounds like early Pinter. Whether those children could have devised such a barrage of questions without the benefit of the role play structure the teacher devised is very unlikely; certainly it is an example of the 'rule of trust'. The teacher is noticeable only in that she has conceived the situation and created an awareness within the children so that they respect – and listen to – each other.

Awareness of social change

Reading, writing, talking and listening – it is familiar ground. Has the world really changed in the 1980s? Arguably, there are two fundamental differences about the teaching of English in the present decade: firstly, an almost hostile – certainly suspicious – questioning of the prevailing emphasis on literature; and secondly, a recognition that changes in society must shift the curriculum if our classrooms are to remain alive. Complicating the issue is the fact that the first of these differences has been foisted upon teachers of English from outside, while the second is more self-generated, if not self-imposed. In practice, of course, it can mean a more 'relevant' curriculum, but 'relevant' to what? To whom? And who acts as judge about such decisions?

The first of these two differences stems from a growing sense of unease felt by employers about the ability of young people to manipulate language for their purposes. The underlying assumption is that the teaching of English is merely concerned with providing children with the necessary skills to 'earn' employment. I have listened (with impatience and disbelief) to an employer certain in his own mind that 'English' should have no part in any TVEI proposal – or, indeed, anywhere else for that matter: it is airy-fairy and therefore expendable . . . give them 'problem solving' and 'decision making' instead. Or 'communication skills': what *is* communication if it isn't reading, writing, talking and listening? What matters most is *why* the communication is necessary; then considerations of appropriateness and the rest become significant. At worst, a 'Communication Skills' syllabus can decontextualise language use and take us into a bleak world where literature is shorn off – as if there really was an age when adolescents don't respond to books any more. Pre-vocational courses must be more than a teeth-gritting exercise in fitting kids for jobs, not least because so many manifestations of life after school are currently so bleak. 'Work' can mean a niche, for a while, on the Maestro assembly line at Cowley, screwing rubber buffers on to the car's tailgate and then fixing earths to the car's rear wheel arches: 'At the end of his eight hour day . . . he will have put in 1,792 screws and fixed 492 buffers and 938 earths in 246 cars.'[27] Or worse, it can be unobtainable and leave you desperate: 'I'm thirty-seven,' says Yosser Hughes in one episode of Alan Bleasdale's *The Boys from the Blackstuff*, 'and I've got nowhere to go.'

'English' courses that masquerade as skills-based units geared only to the world of work should be viewed with great suspicion. This is not because we should neglect our responsibilities in equipping pupils with such skills, but because there are *other* skills which should be fostered, to do with personal development and life beyond work – and, not least, because 'Communication Skills' can most effectively be learned by engaging the hearts and minds of children through literature:

> . . . there's limited time for English on the timetable so we've got to choose what is likeliest to motivate the child and engage her feelings, thoughts, imagination . . . good literature is the most effective, precise, ordered form of language [and thus] it probably gives the best kind of preparation for mastering the practical uses of language.[28]

Teachers of English, apart from resisting the more mindless and bull-headed advances from outside their schools and classrooms, must become involved in the process of adapting the English curriculum to ensure that it reflects the rapid changes in our society. This will mean incorporating more fully into the curriculum material concerned with anti-racist education; film, television and media studies; language awareness; gender, etc.

The black experience

'There is a strong underlying view that black experience is, intrinsically, not as interesting as white experience' – so Rosa Guy remarked recently.[29] To someone like me, raised from an early age on Biggles, Blyton and Arthur Ransome, it does seem that most children's literature is based on the experience of white, middle-class males. (The *NATE Bulletin*, spring 1983, reporting on a conference 'Through Women's Eyes', quoted the following example: the black female African writer Buchi Emecheta 'had a teacher in Lagos with an Oxford MA who used to read them Rupert Brooke. "I'm going to be a writer," said Buchi. "Go to the chapel and pray," responded the teacher, sternly'!)

Teachers can alter their department's policy on multi-cultural literature in a number of ways:

- changing the guidelines that operate for book selection, for both class and library use;

- checking the current bookstock and removing books that the department considers racist;

- devising ways of getting children interested in literature from other cultures.

Choosing texts

Figure 8   A short reading list of Caribbean and African texts

			Which year group?
CARIBBEAN			
Wide Sargasso Sea	Jean Rhys	Penguin (1968)	5–6
The Dragon Can't Dance	Earl Lovelace	Longman (Drumbeat) (1981)	6
The Lonely Londoners	Samuel Selvon	Longman (Drumbeat) (1979)	4–6
Ways of Sunlight	Samuel Selvon	Longman (Drumbeat) (")	4–6
A Brighter Sun	Samuel Selvon	Longman (Drumbeat) (")	4–6
Miguel Street	V. S. Naipaul	Heinemann (CWS) (1974, 1980)	
The Young Warriors	V. S. Reid	Longman (Horizon) (1979)	
New Ships (poetry)	ed. D. G. Wilson	Oxford University Press (1975)	
AFRICAN – short stories			
No Sweetness Here	Ama Ata Aidoo	Longman (Drumbeat) (1980)	4–6
Land Without Thunder	Grace Ogot	East African Publishing House	4–6
Potent Ash	L. Kibera and S. Kahiga	East African Publishing House (1968)	4–6
Secret Lives	Ngugi waThiong'o	Heinemann (AWS) (1975)	4–6
Some Monday for Sure	Nadine Gordimer	Heinemann (AWS) (1975)	5–6
Nine African Stories	Doris Lessing	Longman (1968)	4–6
A Walk in the Night (novella)	Alex LaGuma	Heinemann (1968)	4–6
The River Between (novel)	Ngugi	Heinemann (1965)	5–6
Going Down River Road (novel)	Meja Mwangi	Heinemann (1976)	4–6
Tell Freedom (autobiography)	Peter Abrahams	Allen & Unwin (1968)	4–6

Departments could usefully read several of the books on the list in figure 8 and then discuss their relevance so far as the children in their school are concerned. Subsequently, time can be set aside to consider criteria for selecting texts to use in the classroom.[30]

Books could be chosen deliberately to present the Third World as having:

- characters with whom children can identify;

- characters who are in a position to make decisions that affect their own lives;

- customs, life-styles and culture that exist in their own right;

- heroes whose influence is clearly demonstrated;

- the right to secure their own freedom;

- as strong a self-image as white children;

- a history which does not necessarily have the same perspective as, for example, European countries;

- a language which should be respected and valued for itself. Additionally, family relationships should be presented 'in a warm and supportive manner'; the role of women in shaping Third World history should be accurately represented.[31]

There are, of course, other criteria which we adopt, either consciously or not, when it comes to deciding 'what book'. Above all, the book should be able to 'speak to' children's perceptions of the world, and in the process of reading it the children's view of themselves and the world they move in should be extended and deepened. Until recently, the nearest most children could expect to get to the 'black experience' was E. R. Braithwaite's *To Sir With Love*, a novel in which the black teacher overcomes distrust and resentment, weaning his white class away from racist attitudes by dint of patient, dignified example. However there are different perspectives and wider issues:

Teacher: Does your Dad come from the West Indies?
Lester: Yeah, but I don't feel as though I'm West Indian though.
Teacher: Why?
Lester: Well ... because I was born over here and ... Ah, I feel as though I should adopt the culture of the country I'm in.

Teacher: But don't you like some of the things and specialised
            things of the West Indies, like music?
Lester: How can I, sir? I've never seen the West Indies, I never
            even smelt, touched or heard the West Indies. So I'm
            forced to adopt something near me. You said West
            Indian music, I like it yes, but when I enjoy something I
            need it home bred, you know, near to me. (*Looking at
            each other for a long time.*)
Teacher: Yes but I still think the West Indian culture is more
            interesting.
Lester: Our culture was made interesting by our sweat and
            blood in the cotton fields.[32]

Old Father

Old Father to England in Winter '59.
Cold bite him hard,
Make him bawl in his small basement room
By the Grove.
Evey day he cry out:
'Man, a tekkin' de nex' boat back home.'
But come spring
Old Father still there.

Time passed.
Old Father feet begin to shift.
His roots have no meaning now.
He straighten his hair,
Press it smooth.
Coloured girls no good for he –
Day after day you see him
Bouncing down the road with a blonde,
Never brunette,
And his suit, cream or beige,
Never anything dark.

Old Father don't mix with the boys
On Saturday night no more –
No, he sits in the pub up the road –
The one at the corner
That don't like serving black people –

And he crack joke with them white people on we.
'Tut tut', he would say,
'Isn't it disgusting
How they make a spectacle of themselves
At cricket matches.'

He don't say 'Hello' no more,
Don't eat dasheen or yam –
'not very digestible' –
And Heaven forbid,
He even turn his back on
Saltfish with 'chove an' dumpling.

Boy,
Old Father don't want to know we now,
In his white Rover,
With his slicked-back hair.
And them white people saying
'He's an example to his people.'

Hugh Boatswain[33]

There is a wealth of exciting, provocative writing by black writers that
all English departments should be aware of. Someone in the department
needs to unlock the treasure-house if no one has yet looked inside. One
of the most interesting discussions I've heard in recent months was
about a James Berry poem, 'Brixton Market'. The poem was on this
occasion the focus of a computer program – 'Developing Tray'[34] –
where a small group discusses a poem to which they give shape by
predicting what the writer has put; it is, in fact, the ultimate deletion
exercise – Super-Cloze! Berry's use of dialect flummoxed the group at
first, but the marriage of the program and the issues raised by the poem
(black youths in confrontation with white police) produced talk that was
vibrant and open. It was particularly exciting to see whites instinctively
understanding the Creole but, more significantly, identifying with the
black experience. The fresh view of the world is such an important
consequence of reading black literature in school. It is a contentious
area: the Council of British Pakistanis' criticism of Jan Needle's 'My
Mate Shofiq' is a disturbing example: 'Shofiq' is appearing in English
lessons with increasing regularity, and yet the council objected to ' . . .
its uncorrected stereotypes, its offensive language and its inaccurate
portrayal of the Pakistani way of life and religion.' It is, we are told,
deeply offensive to Muslims. However, the issues are ones we should
not ignore; they offer experiences and perceptions from which pupils of
all backgrounds can learn more about each other and themselves.

The territory is vast:

The old man said, 'Well, you should haveam here already! After all, you is
man now, boy, and you must haveam drink in house for when friend
come.'
   Tiger thought, To my wife, I man when I sleep with she. To bap, I man
if I drink rum. But to me, I no man yet.

Samuel Selvon, *A Brighter Sun*

Tahir wasn't scared of anyone and he'd say, 'Get out, swine,' because those were the only swear words in English that he knew. He didn't speak English very much and when my dad met him on the stairs or invited him round for a cup of tea he'd just say, 'It is very kind, don't trouble, please don't trouble.'

Farrukh Dhondy, *East End at Your Feet*[35]

Charlie: Is different – A whole lot different. In them times so when we went Barbados or Jamaica to play cricket they used to treat us like hogs, boy. When we went on tours they put we in any ole kind of boarding house. The best hotels was for them and the half-scald members of the team – So in Twenty-seven when we was on tour in Jamaica I cause a stink, boy. I had had enough of them dirty little boarding house rooms. I said either they treat me decent or they send me back. The stink I made got into the newspapers. They didn't send me back. But that was the last intercolony series I ever play. They broke me, boy.

Epf
(quietly):   Fer that?

Charlie: I should of known mey place.

Errol John, *Moon on a Rainbow Shawl*[36]

Themes vary enormously, though the extract from Errol John's play, written as long ago as 1958, is close to the heart of it all. 'I should of known mey place,' says Charlie, who has been broken by the inter-island racial jealousy and tension. This theme touches us all, and children will readily acknowledge it. An English department whose work and influence do not reflect the black experience in a multi-cultural society denies children a chance to understand, share and explore the shifting world outside school. A diet of fiction and poetry that reflects only part of that world – white, middle-class images in the mirror – is not enough; instead school bookshelves should include writers like Selvon, Dhondy, Ngugi, Salkey, Emecheta, Narayan, Bernard Ashley (*The Trouble with Donovan Croft*), Jan Needle, Robert Leeson (*Silver's Revenge*), Julius Lester, Rosa Guy, Tony Drake, Rukshana Smith, James Berry, Linton Kwesi Johnston, Wole Soyinka, Athol Fugard, De Larrabeiti (*The Borribles go For Broke*), V. S. Reid. Farrukh Dhondy, in a recent *Times Educational Supplement* article,[37] remarked that 'the subject matter of schooling should have something to do with the "culture" of the schooled.' Our classrooms reflect many cultures, and the work that fills them should recognise that.

CASE STUDY: WORKING WITH MULTI-CULTURAL LITERATURE

The teacher:

You can lump the books into categories – non-racist books written in other parts of the world. Then there's books which attempt to describe another experience (there are so many books about slavery!). Black kids and white kids *like* books about slavery, but I worry that the victim is *always* black. For all that, black kids I've spoken to about it don't want to forget slavery – it happened and it should be remembered.

The third category is books that are written specifically for the multi-cultural market. Strangely, twelve seems to be the significant age – until then, books seem not to deal with race as an issue. The names may be changed, but little else. After twelve, it's all grim reality, police harassment and racial violence – it must be confusing for kids and there seems little help for them in mapping out ways by which they might grab some power for themselves. In the end, I feel it's depressing to be constantly confronted with confrontation. Perhaps there's a hole in the market for racial harmony books . . .

As part of the project I worked with small groups of children, usually about six, chosen by the teacher on the principle of 'two able, two average, two weak'. One of the hidden benefits of the project was how well these weak readers developed. Some of the books were read by individuals within the group, but other books were shared by all of us and, I suppose, 'taught' by me! Bernard Ashley's four stories (*I'm Trying to Tell You*) were much liked. Asian kids enjoyed scenes of Asian life at home, although the white kids failed to comment positively. There's a typical scene in Gillian Cross's *The Runaway* where the Asian mother spreads sari material all over the lounge floor and obviously it's an experience common to Asian children.

One of the teachers I've worked with (in an urban secondary modern) has really turned some of her kids into voracious readers. Do you know how? She's got, as a feature in her room, a large, changing stock of fiction – she makes excellent use of the Library Service. She also reads the books herself and she can match book to child. They also see *her* read. The only sad thing is she's leaving and one of her class said to me the other day: 'I don't go to any library any more because Miss Webb knows what I like.' What'll happen when she leaves at the end of term?

As a result of working in the project, I became much less afraid of taking risks – for the first time I felt able to talk openly about racism in the classroom.

The child (Marjit):

But he shouldn't have written about the bad things. Children are sometimes unpleasant about colour and the way they talk and dress. Most of England is English people and there's not many Pakistanis and Sikhs. Like it sometimes happens in school when they wear Indian clothes like they sometimes do when their others are in the wash. People say they're baggy and 'Where are your proper clothes?' and things – and about the way they talk and their parents and things.[38]

A man's duty?

What do we do with a language like English that has its pronouns so relentlessly gendered?[39]

'There's a funny smell,' said Audrey . . . 'I want to go home.'
'Go then. There's probably other dead 'uns in the wood . . .'
'I knew a girl wouldn't be any *GOOD*.'
. . . Chas threw himself across Audrey protectively. It was a man's duty.[40]

It is not a difficult exercise to monitor and collect examples of sexist language and attitudes. It is scarcely a matter of surprise that staffrooms and classrooms are as male dominated as the rest of society. After all, most headteachers are men. A recognition of the limitations of the niche male society has carved for women is growing – though, often, men who acknowledge such awareness slip into flippant amusement. A male reporter in the *Guardian* (28 April 1984), in a piece under the headline 'Madame Upset by Male Gender', slanted the article neatly and typically:

Mrs Yvette Roudy, the Women's Rights Minister, ticked off a journalist who addressed her this week by her official title, Madame *le* Ministre, when she inaugurated an all-women commission to carry out sex change operations for job-related vocabulary. 'Madame *la* Ministre, s'il vous plaît,' Mrs Roudy said, summing up the commission's role which will be to get rid of male genders for jobs great and small when they are held by women.

The issue goes far deeper than this. It is not just that three times as many men as women are headteachers, that some teachers of both sexes seem incapable of appreciating that girls in school can get a raw deal, and that there are statistics available of which the British educational system should be ashamed: 77 per cent of the students passing A level Maths are boys. For teachers of English, gender, like race, is an issue which is never far away – in the things we read, debate and write; in the way the classroom is organised; in the very departmental structure. Is it right that a department of eight should consist of seven women and one male head of department? What picture of 'English' is that giving? What perception of the role of women will that convey to the children?

Teacher *A*:

I support equal opportunities as much as the next man [!] but I'm not going to mutilate the English language by telling them to write 'chairperson' and 'he or she' all the time. It's clumsy and pointless: we need to concentrate on values and practical issues, not muck about with language.

Teacher *B*:

The only books available for this week's topic consistently use 'man' or 'mankind' for people. Do you use them and ignore it, or confront this use of language, or make the effort to prepare alternative materials? Checking with other teachers, you find out that almost all the main books used by your department do the same: they also give exclusively male examples of human activity except for standard female stereotypes – mother, (house) wife, nurse, secretary, etc. Pictures and illustrations reinforce this bias.

Both the teachers above work in the same department. What are the different implications of teacher *A* or teacher *B* being head of department?

CASE STUDY: EQUAL OPPORTUNITIES IN THE CLASSROOM

My head of department (a man) has always been a bit suspicious of my motives: it's never stated, but his manner invariably suggests that the male members of the department are the 'career teachers'. The rest of us are affected by the pin-money/maternity leave syndrome! I felt strongly that an attitude like that can reinforce the children's stereotyped view of women. Our school is fairly rigid like that, the boys and girls always sit apart; they're listed separately in the registers (boys first!); the books the department buys usually have a male protagonist and, most revealing of all, some rudimentary research that we've done suggests that our teachers tend to teach the boys and ignore the girls. Certainly, the boys in many of our classes expect to get all the attention. Despite his quite blatant opinion that such anxieties stemmed from female whimsy, my head of department readily agreed for the issue to be discussed at a department meeting, but having identified the problem and moved towards *some* kind of awareness at least, the difficulty lay in knowing how best to shift our teaching style – and the material we handled – to put theory into practice.

Second-year group: average to above-average in ability

Time	Plan
Week 1	
Monday 1.2.	(i) Use a variety of games to raise the issue, e.g. 'My Son, My Son'. Working in small groups, ask the pupils to put into the proper order the following story which is cut into separate sections:

There was a road accident.
A lorry ran over a man and his son.
The father was killed outright.
The boy was taken to hospital.
The surgeon at the hospital recognised him.
'My son,' cried the surgeon, horrified, 'that's my son.'

(The booklet/resource pack[41] from which this is taken has a lot of activities that can be built into a programme like this.) Discuss the story.

(ii)   Still in groups, ask the children to list ten occupations that are predominantly female.

(iii)   Discuss.

(iv)   Give each group (six in all) a separate task:

(a)   Devise a questionnaire to seek out the attitudes of the rest of the class and of other groups.

(b)   A survey of 'equality of opportunities' both in and outside school.

(c)   Write (after improvisation?) a play in which a sequence of scenes demands that the audience judge various 'equality issues'.

(d)   Rewrite a story from a woman's point of view.

(e)   Collect pictures, news stories and extracts from literature that show the extent of inequality.

(f)   Invent a marriage contract.

Conclude by reading 'Petronella', a story in which Petronella, 'a tall handsome girl with flaming red hair', rescues Prince Ferdinand, whose idea of fun is 'sunning himself and working at a crossword puzzle ... "What's selfish in nine letters?"   "You   are,"   snapped Petronella.'[42]

Wednesday 5.6   (i)   Continue with group activities.

(ii)   Look at and discuss 'All My Friends are Married Now' by Barbara Child (in *The Gender Trap* by Carol Adams and Rae Laurikietis, and 'The Choosing' by Liz Lochead in *Strictly Private*.

(iii)   Begin reading *Bridge to Terabithia* by Katherine Paterson.

Friday 8   Continue reading.

Week 2

Monday 1.2.   Continue with the above.
Wednesday 5.6
Friday 8.

Week 3
Monday 1.2   Mount a wall display of the groups' findings.

Wednesday 5.6   Finish *Bridge to Terabithia*
Friday 8

Week 4
Monday   Follow up *Bridge.*
Wednesday   Invite in outside speaker (Women's refuge? Peace camp?).
Friday   Begin extended individual writing projects.

What happened?
- Success – the introduction; the poetry; Paterson's novel.
- Limited success – the group work; the display; the outside speaker.
- Failure – the time scale.
- Doubts? – How this experience should be extended.

The quality of the writing that emerged from the month worried me most; while the talk flourished and the novel touched and moved us all, there seemed little to show for it at the end. My head of department was sniffy about this, though he mellowed when he listened to tapes of the children discussing the ending of *Bridge to Terabithia*. Perhaps the group activities were introduced too soon and would have been better if the kids had seemed to be in at their conception.

The place of Media Studies

They do give you a choice of Cultural and Creative subjects. So I have chosen Media Studies (dead easy, just reading newspapers and watching telly) and Parentcraft (just learning about sex, I hope.)
            The Secret Diary of Adrian Mole Aged 13¾ by Sue Townsend

CASE STUDY: 'IMAGE EDUCATION'

I started teaching in London in the early 70's. It was a film post ostensibly, at least that's what the advert said. In fact, it turned out to be English, Remedial and something called Integrated Studies – whatever *that* was, it was nothing to do with film or media studies. There were no resources, simple as that. I stayed just the year.

Although I was trained to teach both Film and English, I didn't feel, in this new job that is, that I had enough paper guidance to help me. So I contacted the BFI [British Film Institute]. In the end, though, it all came down to me. I can remember boning up on film criticism and even trying to get into structuralism and semiotics, thinking it could be used in some way in the classroom. The more down-to-earth side of me, though, was worried about the acceptability of it all. That meant examinations – so I devised a Mode 3 syllabus. It was, I freely admit, done to impress; all that jargon sounds awful now. All done for the exam board's benefit! Luckily, the head was very supportive –

interested too. I can't remember exactly how he phrased it, but he said something like, 'What you've got to do is prove yourself.' Well, I got a scale 2 at the end of the year and some decent capitation, enough to buy some expensive hardware. I guess the six grade 1s impressed the head!

(It's a poignant footnote that the equipment was destined to be buried in a cupboard once this teacher left. I discovered this by chance talking to another teacher from the school years later; he described finding 'a whole load of video equipment in the back of the drama store'.)

About this time I got myself made i/c Audiovisual Resources for the school, so I had ready access to the VCR and I persuaded the Head that we needed to buy a camera. This was about 1976. From now on we were making video film, with, of course, instant playback. Inevitably, that changed my whole way of teaching.

You see, up till then TV had been regarded as 'moving wallpaper', but I wanted to get kids to be critical. I remember the magazine *Screen Education* about that time did a piece on *The Sweeney* and it nudged me into using about six different episodes of the programme – great fun. We spent time looking at the technical vocabulary of film, and demonstrating it with a camera. Certainly, at that time I was more interested in teaching Film. Apart from anything else, my timetable so far as English was concerned was fairly second-rate. Bottom sets and not much exam work.

Then the Head of Drama left and I took over his 5th year; that was what led me into marrying Film and Drama. We were filming improvisations and then discussing them, but that was only a part of it all. 'Image Education' I felt was really important. After all, someone's done some research in the United States which claims that, by the age of ten, kids have seen 11,000 murders on television, and without much thinking going on.

What sort of things did I do? Some were quite simple really. I asked the kids to tear a hole in a piece of A4 paper and, after looking through it, to describe the world they see. It's fascinating; you're soon into a realisation that wherever you put the hole is the perspective. It begins to dawn on kids that someone makes decisions about who sees what – and how you see it. Because we couldn't afford enough film, we used devices like the comic strip and discussed how it was that losing just one frame can alter the story. I was intrigued by how many stories you can tell with one set of pictures – and then, of course, you're into the whole business of the news and the manipulation of truth! I got a set of forty-eight pictures of a teachers' demonstration – from the Society for Education in Film and TV, through the BFI – and got the kids to tell the story from the teachers' point of view, and then from the other side. Which is TRUE? The pictures don't change, just the chosen sequence and the voice-overs. What made it even more bizarre was that I was actually on that demonstration, so there was *my* perception of the events too!

I want to make children aware of broader issues. In the mid-seventies the prevalent style in the teaching of Media Studies was the 'inoculation approach'; you know, that the principal reason for teaching it was to countermand the media's harmful effect upon society. I think now we can be more positive than that. For a start, the media *are* a significant element in all our lives and to the children themselves, well, the image is more important than the written word. English becomes Communication, but much, much more than the BEC/TEC type of 'Communication Skills'.

We did a lot of work looking critically at films. They were ordered, fairly cheaply, from the BFI and we even specialised – Hitchcock movies for instance. Time was a problem; the fact that I had just four periods a week with them meant that I tended to concentrate on certain aspects of the film, We'd look, for instance, at the opening sequence. I think that was wrong, on reflection. We should have looked at the whole film and then focused down on particular issues. The fact that the school had set up a Film Society for the parents helped too – generating interest, as well as providing a further opportunity for booking films.

When I moved schools after five years, it was very difficult to start again. Once again there were no resources – it was a reminder of how new it all was. When I went to my first exam board meeting there were only six schools involved from right across southern England. I'd been appointed as a Head of Drama, operating within the English Department and, for me, Drama now took first place.

Now that I'm Head of my own English Department, I'm beginning to think again about the significance of Media work within English. Mainstream English must be my main priority and the Drama matters too. We're a small, overstretched department, dealing with CSE/O/A English; CSE/O Drama; City and Guilds and CEE, but the intention, next year, is to bring a Media element in within a revamped fourth-year curriculum. It'll be just a part of a new modular approach, masquerading as 'Image Education'. I suppose that as Head of Department I can give it a status that a decade ago I had to derive from examination respectability. And I've got my hands on the purse strings now! Over the next few years, I want to spend time trying to integrate all of this into a more coherent approach to English; looking at the way visual and linguistic messages are coded. It's a question of deconstructing and then building it up again.

Paul Rhodes, Head of English at a 13–18 comprehensive school in Windsor, has clearly shifted ground since he launched into developing the potential of film in the classroom.

- What importance – what balance of time, for example – would you place on the proposed module of 'Image Education' in the fourth-year curriculum?
- What are the implications for the curriculum in the preceding years – and not just in secondary school?

When the curriculum fails . . .

Some months ago, a school I know was the subject of a General Inspection by HMI. One pinstripe-suited Inspector was sitting in on a lesson with a group of fifth-year 'low attainers'; he was at the back of the class, writing detailed notes in a DES-monogrammed notebook. One of the lads turned to him, sniffed and then said, with perfect timing in a momentary (and unusual) silence, 'I could do that – gi' us a job!' The story has some interesting implications: Alan Bleasdale's biting dramas of life for the unemployed on Merseyside were part of that 'remedial' boy's world. It is too easy to pin the labels 'remedial' and 'low attainers' on children for whom the school's curriculum has little real meaning. Teachers of English are lucky in that we, more than anyone, have the scope within our subject to range over the children's world, its language, its customs and injustices. English teaching in the 1980s must not mirror Jack Common's experience at the turn of the century:

> We learn reading and boredom, writing and boredom, arithmetic and boredom, and so on according to the curriculum, till in the end it is quite certain you can put us to the most boring job there is and we'll endure it.[43]

3 Language:Diversity, Awareness and Policies

> You know what my grandmother said about Ernest Bevin? She said: 'They can't make him foreign secretary. He's got a Bristol accent.'

The experience of the playwright Peter Nicholls – or, more correctly, his grandmother – echoes that of many people: language may be all-powerful, but some language is more powerful than others. W. S. Tomkinson's *The Teaching of English* (1921), quoted in the opening chapter, had a clear and uncomplicated view of the problem:

> Nothing but sustained, conscious and scientific effort will root out a native pronunciation, and often men of considerable education carry their native accent to the grave ... It may be asked what standard of pronunciation we are to aim at. There is no absolute standard. A reasonable guide is the pronunciation of cultured people.

Presumably a definition of a cultured person was one whose standard of pronunciation was irreproachable! Of course, it all depends whose culture ...

Once attention is focused on the nature of people's language and its correctness/appropriateness, we are into contentious territory. One way to begin, or reopen, a staff debate over language is to ask a whole staff to 'mark' the same piece of children's writing and then analyse the points of difference: as an exercise it immediately exposes the 'language prejudice' of the staff,[1] their individual perceptions of what is 'correct'. The issue is one that will not go away; indeed, the likelihood is that English departments will increasingly be at the sharp end of the discussion as pressure increases for a fundamental change in the English curriculum. The battleground is familiar. A review by David Crystal of John Honey's pamphlet *The Language Trap: Race, Class and the 'Standard English' Issue in British Schools* in a recent edition of *English in Education*[2] is an example of the passion aroused by the issue.

There are, bound up in the chapter's title, two (perhaps three) aspects: the question of 'diversity', the varieties of English which should be encouraged and developed in the classroom; this is linked with 'awareness', the process by which children are made aware, or come to an awareness of what language is and what it is capable of; and language policy, the rigorous path towards establishing a school's policy for – 1970s phrase coming up! – 'language across the curriculum'.

'Language across the curriculum' revisited

Most schools seem now to have convinced themselves that 'language across the curriculum' is either outmoded or sunk without trace, so it may be appropriate to begin there. The English department has a role and responsibility in developing a policy for language which makes sense and which makes the learning experiences of children more relevant and more deep-seated, closer to them. The pamphlet *Bullock Revisited*, which appeared in June 1982, questioned not the principle, but the strategy schools had been encouraged to pursue by the *The Bullock Report*. The pamphlet opined that the way forward in practice 'may be achieved through . . . the process of self-evaluation and improvement: that of asking each department to review its aims, objectives, methods and achievements in teaching its specialist subject'.[3] In passing, it muses on the importance of new developments in examinations helping to shift teacher attitudes to language:

> . . . no doubt it would help if the examination syllabuses of some subjects for GCE and CSE were to demand less factual recall and more evidence of understanding. Moreover, if marking of papers for examinations in all subjects at these levels included, and was known to include, deduction of marks for poor English or addition of marks for good English, this would provide a powerful incentive for teachers generally to give more attention to their pupils' use of language. Planning for the introduction of new examinations at 16+ might valuably include such considerations.

This doesn't seem very helpful. It appears to ignore the importance – the predominance – of language in learning, and appears more concerned with 'good English', the label which means so many different things to different people. What attitude would the author of *Bullock Revisited* take to Ernest Bevin's Bristol accent?

Some years ago, Peter Medway and Mike Torbe wrote an article in *The Times Educational Supplement*[4] describing their experience of the Canadian move towards 'language across the curriculum'. At one point they identify the central idea of language and learning in this way:

> [It is] that we *make* knowledge as we talk, write, listen and read . . . [this] is a hard one to grasp, because it flies in the face of common sense, which tells us that language is so essential to education because all that knowledge has to be communicated from those who know it to those who do not.

In fact, the central idea is not difficult to grasp; what is difficult is the process of reflecting upon that central idea and then questioning how it accords with an individual subject teacher's style in the classroom. The mismatch between the two can give rise to a variety of responses, but much will depend on the ethos of the school: whether major issues like this can be tackled in a spirit of tentative enquiry and collaboratively across subject barriers; or whether the normal mode is to put up the shutters and sit tight until the questions and doubts have disappeared. Hoping that individual subject departments can grapple with the issues in their own review of performance can work only in departments where there is an underlying spirit of enquiry fuelled by concern to 'get it right'. What happens in departments where the only questions are on the level of 'Can I borrow some chalk'?

English teachers are used to being treated and regarded as the school's walking dictionary. Inevitably, the 'language policy' has frequently landed at the door of the English Department or, more precisely, as the last item on a Head of English department's job description. Unless this organisational problem has been resolved, there is no fruitful way forward. Only if the Head of English has the overt support of the Head, and the *practical* involvement of a deputy head and a working group from other departments, can the exercise (horrible word!) achieve any tangible results that will affect the children's experience as they wander through the day from classroom to classroom. At the same time, a powerful English department, certain of its direction and mutually supportive, can play a vital part in raising questions in people's minds about the processes of learning through language. To begin with, English teachers will have much to offer in developing staff awareness about the reading environment, learning through writing, the potency of talk and the need to develop listening skills.

Encouraging staff involvement

(1) The suggestion has already been made about comparing staff response to the same piece of writing (see page 48) – a process, incidentally, which has also been used successfully with school governors. A development of that strategy is to collect all the writing done by two students over one week in all subjects and then for small, interdepartmental groups to discuss what picture of learning the collated writing presents. Such an exercise can throw up some invaluable and disturbing findings. One school, which had deliberately focused on 'an able child' and on a student 'just above remedial', identified (in five minutes!) a range of issues that raised questions about the school's policy for language:

- The children (Louise, the successful learner, and Wayne) seemed to be cast very much in the role of passive receivers of knowledge.

- Both children's standard of presentation varied markedly from lesson to lesson or, more pertinently, teacher to teacher.

- There was a feeling that Louise's neatness prejudiced teachers in her favour, while Wayne's scrawl merely antagonised.

- Was Louise being 'stretched' sufficiently?

- Was the curriculum relevant to them? Wayne, for example, a fourteen-year-old struggling with his native language, was following a very academic course in German.

- Wayne had written substantially more than Louise during the week.

(2) In general, it is less threatening to examine the *pupils'* classroom experience than to home in at once on teacher style and performance. Following an individual pupil, or a class, around the school for one day is another illuminating strategy, presenting a realistic overview of what the children enjoy/suffer. One such inquiry with a first-year group opened up the whole area of differing staff attitudes to boys and girls: one member of the language working party had stayed with one class throughout the day, noting down each time a pupil made a positive verbal contribution to the lesson. The figures suggested two main causes for concern: that boys caught the teacher's eye far more often than girls; and that some children went through the day without so much as raising an arm to answer a question – or failing to speak at all.

Case study: one school's developing policy of language.
Although the tangible result of the protracted debate was a weighty 'policy document', it was the process itself that mattered and is more likely to keep the momentum rolling.

THE PROCESS

September	Head keen to raise standards of literacy (his phrase!). Memo to Heads of Department instructing them to ensure that *all* staff mark children's language errors. Head of English, anxious about superficiality, suggests thorough review of the role of language in learning.
October	Head of English talks to English Department. Questionnaire produced (figure 9).
November	85% response (voluntary) to questionnaire. Working paper drawn up by English Department.
December	Staff discussion of working paper: small groups chaired by staff from various departments (not heads of departments).

Figure 9   Questionnaire

The working party's expectations are included in the right hand column

1	How do you, in your particular subject, allow for the importance of language in learning?	Language's relationship with thought . . .
2	What kind of balance do you think there ought to be between writing, listening and talking in your subject?	Presupposes structure in planning for language activity.
3	Do you yourself see language in your classroom and your particular subject as (a) a means of transmission of knowledge from teacher to pupil OR (b) a means of interpretation of new and unfamiliar ideas in terms of what is already known?	Progressive ◄──────► Traditional Teaching Style
4	Do your lessons provide sufficient opportunity for pupils to rework – in talk and/or writing – the information you wish to convey? If yes, please explain 'how' in some detail.	The only way to make knowledge theirs.
5	How important is the use of worksheets in your subject?	Intended to focus attention on the problems of using worksheets.
6	Are the worksheets part of a strategy involving the teacher or are they selfcontained teaching strategies in themselves?	
7	Has group work (up to six pupils) any function/value in your subject? Please explain fully.	Importance of TALK.
8	In your opinion, what sort of difficulties constitute a 'language problem'?	Is it *language* or *subject*?
9	To whom, if anyone, would you refer a pupil with a language problem?	Back to oneself? Pastoral staff? Remedial dept?
10	How important do you feel the marking of errors in spelling, punctuation and expression to be?	Depends on the child.
11	Have you any strategies for marking pupils' work?	What do you *value*?
12	Who should be concerned to develop and extend a pupil's vocabulary?	Everyone!
13	What special reading demands does your subject make?	Mixed ability problems.
14	Is the reading material that is offered to pupils sufficiently clear to them?	Selection of text
15	Do you teach reading in your particular subject? What help do you give in comprehension?	Distinction drawn between 'reading' and 'comprehension'.
16	To what extent do you feel the English Department should be responsible for pupils' accuracy of expression?	Talk and Writing.
17	Do you see any value in examining the use of 'language across the curriculum' and developing a common policy for the school? Please be explicit!	

January	Staff Meeting. Visiting speaker stressed:

           (i)   Need for variety of teaching method.
           (ii)   Redrafting in learning to write and in learning.
           (iii) Need for a marking policy.
           (iv)   Need for varied reading.
           (v)   Value of talk.

February   In–service: school closed for half a day. Staff looking at the questionnaire and responses; focusing on the reality of classroom experience.

March   Head of Department identified seven areas which appeared to concern staff:

- Redrafting.
- *Who* is responsible for language development?
- Common marking policy/correction code.
- Likely attainment levels in language?
- Talk: small group discussion.
- 'Priority' vocabulary.
- Readability of texts.

Non-heads of departments asked to chair working parties on *one* of the above.

April to July   Working parties met.

October   Document produced. Recognition that the work must continue.

Policy documents have a nasty habit of turning yellow and curling at the edges as the sun beats through the staffroom windows. Stick a staple in something, put the school crest on it, ask the Head to write an introduction – and there's every chance that it will be lost without trace. Unless the strategy includes a cross-curricular system for follow-up, monitoring and revision, there is no guarantee that anything will ever change, and certainly all hope of coherence will have disappeared. Once someone has grasped the reins, make sure they don't let go.

The pupils' view

Interestingly, one of the strands the above-mentioned working party pursued was a questionnaire aimed at the *pupils*:

1   In your lessons each day, do you get work which involves you in:

ANSWER YES OR NO	A lot	Quite a lot	Sometimes	Hardly ever	Never
(a) Group work					
(b) Talk/discussion					
(c) Note taking					
(d) Revision					
(e) Redrafting					

2   Which subjects, in your opinion, involve you most in:
    (a)   Group work?
    (b)   Note taking?
    (c)   Revision?
    (d)   Redrafting?

3   (i)   Do you have any preference for any of the above-mentioned
           methods of learning? If yes, say which ones.
    (ii)   Do you know of any other methods of learning?

4   Why do you prefer your chosen method? Can you think of some
    reasons?

5   Do you feel that you achieve less in some subjects because:
    (a)   the subject matter is difficult?
    (b)   the language is which it is expressed is difficult for you to
          understand?
    (c)   Any other reason?

6   Do you think it would improve your understanding and enjoy-
    ment of a subject if the teachers helped you to understand
    (i)   through discussion and exploration?
    (ii)   through the language in which the subject matter is
         expressed?
    (iii) through its specialist vocabulary first?

7   Can you give some reasons why you feel that you are not learning or
    understanding as much as you would like to? List your reasons below
    without mentioning teachers' names:
    (i)
    (ii)
    (iii)
    Other:

The findings (on a very small sample):

1 There was a surprising degree of disagreement as to the nature of activities the children experienced; e.g. some felt they did 'a lot' of group work, while the majority claimed it was 'hardly ever'.
2 (a) Most group work? A wide range of subjects.
   (b) Most note taking? Geography and Science most 'popular' choices.
   (c) Most revision? Maths and Modern Languages most 'popular' choices.
   (d) Most redrafting? English.
3 (i) Preference for learning method: groupwork.
   (ii) Other named methods included: role play, discussion, reading, TV, worksheets.
4 Main reason for preference: 'everyone is involved and different ideas can be shared'.
5 and 6   Answers to 5 and 6 were predictable. Reasons for *not* learning are worth repeating;

- Fear and overstrictness of teachers.
- People in the group put me off.
- Reluctance to ask teacher questions.
- Some teachers are too soft.
- Teachers talk/moan too much.
- Unrealistic expectations by teachers.
- Over-use of big words.
- Lack of clarity.
- Lack of time.
- Classes too big.

And:

- 'More books, so it's not one book between two.'
- 'I'm learning as much as I'd like to'!

Extending language awareness

'There is a busybody on your staff,' George Bernard Shaw wrote to the editor of *The Times* in 1907,

who devotes a lot of time to chasing split infinitives. Every good literary craftsman splits his infinitives when the sense demands it. I call for the immediate dismissal of this pedant. It is of no consequence whether he decides to go quickly, or quickly to go, or to quickly go. The important thing is that he should go at once.

Shaw's Edwardian sexism may jar, but his rational view of one of the traditional grammatical controversies (or is it con*tro*versies?) is reassuring. It isn't that grammar doesn't matter. Professor David Crystal commented recently that 'You can't get away from grammar, *ever!*' Indeed, it was less a comment than an impassioned, enthusiastic defence of language study. He would argue that fostering linguistic awareness in young children is 'bigger' even than reading and writing. If reading and writing are to be significant parts of a child's learning and life, then an excitement and an understanding of the power and beauty of language are prerequisites. Teachers too need to have that same understanding, and there is a dangerous mismatch between what children expect language to be and what teachers think it is. This is more true of slow learners and younger children, but we ought to recognise that language prejudice can work both ways.

Teachers and pupils together
The map of current thinking about language in figure 10 is more a route indicator than detailed ordnance survey. It helps to initiate a discussion within the department about the areas of the map which remain unexplored:

● What functions of language seem important to you? And to the children?

● How can the children be made aware of how English varies in accent, dialect and style?

● To what extent is it useful for children to know about change in language? About the factors that have caused the change?

● What kinds of dialect/accent are most/least acceptable to you?

● What should the department do about children whose first language is not English? What implications does bilingualism have for the curriculum and teaching style?

● If grammar is merely a 'descriptive instrument'[5], should it be used as a tool to develop language?

● 'We judge a register according to its effectiveness as communication and its suitability to a particular situation. Thus we no longer think, as people did formerly, of *one* "correct" English, but of many correct Englishes; we think of "appropriateness" rather than "correctness".[6] Agreed?

Figure 10 Thinking about language

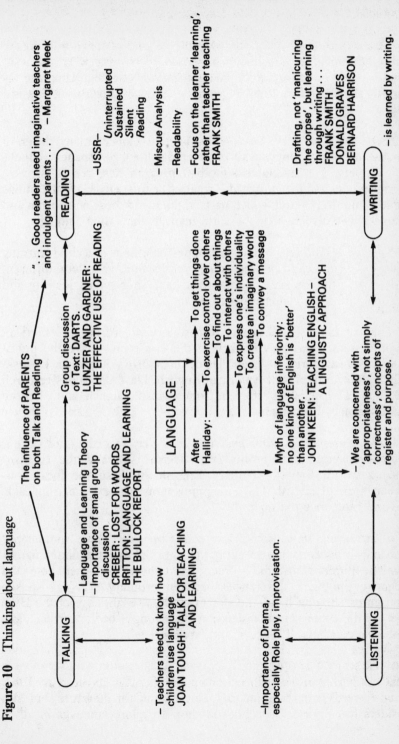

The influence of PARENTS on both Talk and Reading

" . . . Good readers need imaginative teachers and indulgent parents . . . " – Margaret Meek

TALKING

– Teachers need to know how children use language
JOAN TOUGH: TALK FOR TEACHING AND LEARNING

– Language and Learning Theory
– Importance of small group discussion
CREBER: LOST FOR WORDS
BRITTON: LANGUAGE AND LEARNING
THE BULLOCK REPORT

Group discussion of Text: DARTS.
LUNZER AND GARDNER:
THE EFFECTIVE USE OF READING

READING

–USSR– *Uninterrupted Sustained Silent Reading*

– Miscue Analysis
– Readability
– Focus on the learner 'learning', rather than teacher teaching
FRANK SMITH

LANGUAGE

After Halliday:
To get things done
To exercise control over others
To find out about things
To interact with others
To express one's individuality
To create an imaginary world
To convey a message

– Myth of language inferiority: no one kind of English is 'better' than another.
JOHN KEEN: TEACHING ENGLISH – A LINGUISTIC APPROACH

– We are concerned with 'appropriateness', not simply 'correctness', concepts of register and purpose.

–Importance of Drama, especially Role play, improvisation.

LISTENING

WRITING

– Drafting, not 'manicuring the corpse', but learning through writing . . .
FRANK SMITH
DONALD GRAVES
BERNARD HARRISON

–is learned by writing.

" . . . READING, WRITING, TALKING ABOUT WRITING AND TALKING IN ORDER TO WRITE MUST BE CONTINUAL POSSIBILITIES: THEY OVERLAP AND INTERLOCK . . . " FRANK SMITH

Case studies: classroom activities for language awareness[7]
IDEAS FOR FIRST TO FIFTH YEARS
Language treasure hunt – first year Organise a kind of 'town trail' in the neighbourhood of your school, concerned specifically with language. Include examples of foreign languages; international sign language (as on traffic signs); archaic English; pompous English; advertising English; slang; and so on.

(ii) *Every day around the world – second year* Collect many different examples of foreign languages from everyday life – newspapers, chocolate wrappers, bus timetables, football programmes, record sleeves, advertisements, picture postcards, greetings cards, etc. Have the pupils (a) guess and (b) research which parts of the world these come from and compile a wall display, using a world map, to show their findings.

(iii) *Baby talk – third year* Make some tape-recordings of a child learning to talk – the same child between nine months and 2½, or else different children at different ages. Either way, have your pupils identify and categorise the main changes which occur.

(iv) *American English – fourth year* Record an extract from an American TV programme, and play it back in the classroom. Have the pupils identify and categorise all examples of distinctively American English. Collect other examples of American English. Have the pupils research *why* American English is different from 'British' English, and what the main influences have been.

(v) *Dialect dictations – fourth and fifth years* Play recordings of various different dialects, from around the British Isles and the English-speaking world. Include standard English and also the local non-standard form of English. Have the pupils transcribe extracts from each, note and categorise the main differences.

(vi) *What is non-standard? – fourth and fifth years* Make some tape-recordings of local people speaking their normal non-standard English. Have the pupils transcribe extracts from these, and then note and categorise the main differences between ordinary everyday spoken language on the one hand and, for example, the language of the BBC news on the other. Have discussion of 'wrong', 'bad', 'correct', and emphasise concepts of 'dialect' and 'appropriate'.

AN INTER-SCHOOL PROJECT
Paula's department has, since her appointment as its head in 1981, moved towards a curriculum that allows room for literature, but also considers it a priority that children should explore language in all its

forms, that they should be aware of how language is used for various functions. Typically, the unit[8] described below stresses both audience and purpose.

The idea grew from a friendship between Paula and a teacher at one of the local primary schools: they both agreed that they wanted more *real* interaction between the schools. For years, there had been desultory meetings, lists of reading ages dutifully passed on and even, on occasions, exchange-teaching; but they felt that none of these activities made use of the pupils' experiences and perceptions of school. Paula suggested that her third-year group should write stories specifically for seven- and eight-year-old children in the primary school.

First lesson As a class, 3B prepared themselves for the visit to the primary school (where about 50 per cent of them had gone). Paula reminded them of the concept of writing for an audience by looking with them at several examples of professionally written stories for seven- and eight-year-olds. Inevitably, the lesson became a jumble of memories for a while with a number of the children describing their own feelings of five and six years before. Only in the last ten minutes did Paula break the news of the proposed visit to Canford Primary. The children would make their own way there and be without any direct supervision: Paula wanted an element of independence and self-direction.

Second lesson Both teachers had arranged things in such a way that the children mixed freely: the third-years had been asked to take note of things the juniors were interested in and to listen carefully to the way they talked. The conversations were wide-ranging:

- about 'big school' and the differences in their school lives;
- about books and stories the younger children had enjoyed;
- about music, television, older and younger sisters and brothers.

Many of the children from 3B read to the younger ones. All of them looked at the class library and noted down information about those books which were particularly popular. For this session they used a questionnaire, part of which is included here:

Section 1: to pupils   *Pupil's name:*
1 What kind of books do you like reading?
2 What is the name of a book you have enjoyed
   reading recently?
3 What kind of books do you prefer reading?
     (i) Books about animals?
     (ii) Books about people?
     (iii) Books about characters that aren't real (e.g. 'Mr Men')?
4 If you could have a book especially written for you, what would you
   like it to be about?

The purpose of the questionnaire was to focus the pupil's attention on one particular primary child, to whom, hopefully, she/he would later read their completed story.

Third lesson Back at school, 3B spent most of a double lesson browsing through and discussing a variety of books – all fiction – which had been specifically written for the seven- and eight-year-old market.

Fourth lesson Paula concentrated on 'plot' and 'character' and the relationship between the two. The class each invented their own characters and spent time developing that person: appearance, habits, behaviour, etc. Decisions were taken about the practicalities of writing stories; for example, would the story be read *by* the primary school children or *to* them? What degree of difficulty should the book's language have? What sort of illustrations? How many? Would they add to the text or replace it?

Over the next week 3B spent some time involved in redrafting their work, right through to its final production (cover? binding? print?). The cover, in fact, was a large part of one lesson. They considered its role (to attract, inform, etc); they were to be made from card and covered with library film with plastic spiral bindings.

Conclusion Eventually 3B returned to Canford Primary, this time for a whole afternoon. The stories were read, shared and discussed. Paula regarded the 'debriefing' the following day as equally important, when 3B talked through their successes and failures, focusing on language, its impact and its ability to clarify and confuse; to excite and bore; to amuse and sadden. The books themselves remained in Canford's class library. Not the least important element in the activity was the fact that, in the teacher's words,

> ... the actual readings were filmed, using the school's portable video system – and operated by the pupils. This allowed groups to share what had happened even though they had not directly been involved. It also provides a 'springboard' resource when we launch the project next year.

Finally ...

> The living language is like a cow path: it is the creation of the cows themselves, who, having created it, follow it or depart from it according to their whims or their needs.[9]

Language in the English classroom should liberate, not constrain. Language of many kinds should be valued, talked about, taped, listened to and explored; it should never be decontextualised and divorced from meaning. In a broader school context, *all* staff can benefit from shared experience, prejudice and convictions about the role of language in the learning of their own subject disciplines. English teachers, with their sensitivity to language use and their awareness of the children's needs and thinking, are well placed to ensure that a school's move towards a policy for language can have real meaning.

4 Coping with Pressure

English departments have a high pain threshold. Although their classes tend to be larger, the marking load heavier and their teaching spaces inadequately resourced and furnished, the tendency in schools is for senior managers to make particularly exhausting demands upon them. These demands can vary from expectations about schools plays, theatre visits, magazines and debating societies to assumptions that a Head of English is responsible for the school's language, library and study skills programme. English departments can be the focus of concern about a school's policy for marking, about political bias in considering social issues, or about literature that some people would wish to censor.

> In recent years [said Bullock in 1974!] the role of the head of department has grown in complexity. Not only has the subject increased in scope and widely diversified, but greater flexibility has been required of it to meet individual needs and interests . . . [Heads of departments are] experiencing considerable pressures, and they have had insufficient time and help available to them.[1]

Allocation of time

● At least one lesson in seven should be English.

'The Head has suddenly decided to cut us back to four periods a week. Well, you can't do English in four periods a week.' Just as it is unnerving to discover the variations in the length of the school day, so the range in time allocation for English from school to school is a cause for concern. Ten years ago, the Bullock Report struck on the figure of 200 minutes per week as being an acceptable ration, but advice, practice and the pressures on the timetable have all altered considerably since then. The National Association for the Teaching of English recommended, in 1981, that at least one lesson in seven should be English, but HMI and others, notably the Schools Council in *The Practical Curriculum* (1981), had gone for a 10 per cent minimum. A curriculum survey in one authority recently indicated that its schools (for first-year pupils) allocated just over six periods in a forty-period week on average; this figure, however, included Drama and masked a range from four periods to nine! A random group of English teachers drawn from a variety of local education authorities included one teacher whose department were restricted to 160 minutes per week, and another where 210 minutes was the norm.

Such variations make English vulnerable. There are some interesting hints contained within the following comments from a Head of Department who has experienced attempts to restrict the time for English:

> We reacted too late and we were far too isolated – and, of course, both these errors of judgement are inextricably connected. It was the end of June before we recognised the threat and by then the timetable was not only virtually complete, but was showing distinct signs of warp caused by falling rolls. We were overstaffed and that constraint touched everything else. Now that I've moved to my own department, I've made two positive attempts to prevent a similar thing happening. First of all, I've concentrated on communicating the nature of what we do to as many people as possible: other staff and the senior management of course, but also the parents and governors. We've held evenings to share with parents the range and demands of our work and I've spoken to the governors about the department and what it is that we are trying to do. Secondly, I've made a point of keeping close to the timetabler! I don't want to get caught again.

There is a lot to be said for ensuring that there is a *real* and widespread awareness of the rigorous nature of English: ignorance can be alarming and dangerous. *The Times Educational Supplement* of 17 April 1981, which printed the NATE recommendations referred to above, quotes some remarks made by Members of Parliament in response: at least one of them thought that learning to parse sentences was an integral part of the English programme!

What kind of working space?

- 'I can't teach English *there*, Headmaster!'

> Firstly, I'd like the room number, subject and teacher's name to be on the door. The room would be full of whatever the subject was, and have posters, maps, etc. on the walls. I would have the desks arranged so that you could talk or confer with more than three other people, be allowed to walk around the room and be allowed to talk with whoever you like, all during the lesson.

That fourth-year pupil has readily identified two of the fundamental issues about the learning environment: you need space and a sense of permanence. If you want to cramp an English teacher's style, get her or him scurrying from one cluttered broom cupboard to another, preferably every thirty-five minutes through an eight-period day!

English rooms should reflect an individual teacher's style and they should be clustered together, ideally near the library and the space used for Drama. Isolated outposts – huts scattered on the edge of windswept playing fields – are likely to mean that the children who are taught their English in such surroundings get a raw deal. This is partly because no one teacher may have responsibility for the room, and also because the department's resources cannot be to hand; therefore the teacher is forced to carry books, worksheets, paper and tapes through a campus which, for two terms at least, may well be puddled and bleak.

Priorities

What aspects of the 'environment for English' does the department already have? What priority would the department place on the others?

1 Tables and chairs light enough for easy movement.
2 Carpets in all classrooms.
3 Shelving in classrooms.
4 Display facilities (pinboard) on at least two walls.
5 Blackout.
6 Sufficient electrical sockets.
7 Storage facilities in each room.
8 A central store.
9 An easily visible and manoeuvrable chalk/blackboard.
10 A space available for recording purposes (children's small group discussion).
11 Specialist equipment: video, computer, typewriter, cassette recorder, overhead projector.
12 Arrangements of furniture that allow for group work.

Realism in children's fiction

● How far can you go?

> So the trustees of Ohio State were right in 1956 when they canned the English instructor for assigning *Catcher in the Rye* to his freshman class. They knew there is no qualitative difference between the kid who thinks it's funny to fart in chapel, and Che Guevara.
>
> *The Book of Daniel* by E. L. Doctorow[2]

The Headmaster took the visitor's arm and guided him conspiratorially across his office. 'Have a look at what I've got in here!' he said, turning the combination on the safe. The door swung open, revealing a pile of orange-spined paperbacks; the adolescent on the cover of the top copy was executing a grubby-fingered V-sign. 'There you are,' the Head said, 'thirty copies of *Kes* – unused I'm glad to say.' The incident was recounted to me some years ago by a local authority adviser in a county in the East Midlands. Despite the fact, perhaps, that someone has succeeded in liberating those virgin copies of Hines's novel, the question of what is deemed acceptable in terms of literature in the classroom is still very much with us.

Dr Bowdler, in the last century, felt obliged to twist Shakespeare: Amiens's song in Act 2 of *As You Like It* includes the lines, 'Under the greenwood tree / Who loves to lie with me . . .' In Bowdler's version, 'lie' becomes 'work'! In the 1980s, Shakespeare's pre-eminence in the cultural heritage allows him at least to savour violence, sex and *doubles-entendres* with equanimity. There are few English departments, however, where doubts have not been expressed, either from within the department or, more unsettlingly, from outside – by the Head, the governors or 'concerned parents' – about fiction that is perceived to cross the unwritten line between the acceptable and the 'obnoxious' (to quote from one parent's letter which came my way recently). Robert Westall's novel *The Machine Gunners* which has now, rightly, become an established text for second and third years was a focus for argument and, indeed, Bowdlerisation. Jessica Yates's article in *Children, Language and Literature*[3] indicates some of the squeamish censorship that the Puffin editors brought to the text before publishing the 1979 Puffin version:

> 'Frigging fool' *becomes* 'Faffing fool'. 'He bit me, the Nazi sod' *becomes* 'the Nazi swine!' All occasions of the use of 'frigg' and 'frigging' have been cut, but several 'buggers' have been retained when they refer to the Germans en masse!

What would you do if . . . ?

> As he waved me to a chair I caught sight of a paperbacked novel on his desk and guessed why I'd been summoned. [The Head] got his pipe going, pulled his chair closer to the desk and held up the book.
>
> 'You've been giving this as extra reading to some of your second-year 'A' level pupils, I believe.'
>
> 'Yes.'
>
> 'Any particular reason?'
>
> 'It illuminates in a powerful and vivid way an area of life I thought they might be better off knowing about.'
>
> . . . I've had a telephone call from a parent. A long call. He was very upset. He sent his daughter to me with the book on Friday. He says the last place he expects to send filth into his home is school, and certainly not at the instigation of a teacher.'

In Stan Barstow's novel *A Brother's Tale*[4] the Head – after advising the teacher that it might be the right time for a move ('Have you thought of applying for the English Adviser's job when Tom Noonan moves on?') – feels compelled to call in all the offending copies and locks them away. It is a solution to please no one and from which only a lasting distrust and mutual resentment can emerge.

How can such situations be avoided?

- By talking as a department about censorship and 'realism'; by knowing what the team believes in and can defend.

- By knowing how to articulate that defence.

- By sharing with other English departments, advisers, HMI and the Education Library Service perceptions about 'difficult' texts; by knowing other people's accepted boundaries.

- By matching individuals to books with professional care and certainty.

- By knowing *precisely* what it is about a text that needs sharing with children; by knowing why you've chosen it.

- By knowing *precisely* why a book should be 'banned': real examples include objections to the language in *The Machine Gunners* (bugger, sod, bollocks); concern over adolescent sexuality with *Hey Dollface* by Deborah Hautzig or *Basketball Game* by Julius Lester; or rejection of sympathetic treatment of an apparently unappealing protagonist – *Gowie Corby Plays Chicken* by Gene Kemp. (At least three of those four I would want multiple copies of in my department.)

Above all, we should remember what reading should be – and frequently isn't: demanding both emotionally and intellectually; subversive in that it raises questions on matters which we had held to be certain. Good fiction should shake that certainty in us. At the same time, it helps to hold in the mind another view of what reading can be. This was unwittingly expressed in a recent TV interview with failed 1960s millionaire John Bloom who was describing his collapse which had followed that of his empire. 'I saw no one for ten months,' he said. 'I hid in the house and just . . . *read* – I was like a *vegetable*'!

Mixed ability teaching

- 'Send for the stock of early retirement forms!'

One of the pupils who completed the language questionnaire (page 54) commented on her form: 'Pupils who are doing O levels usually get more attention from the teacher than others who are doing CSE exams. I sometimes feel that some teachers have no time for those who find the subject difficult.'

Badly taught, mixed ability cannot benefit anybody. A teacher whose style of classroom management remains untouched by a change to mixed ability is failing to recognise the importance of that change. The preparation and commitment demanded of him or her at this time is unlikely to be equalled by any subsequent change in circumstances throughout a teaching career. As well as a firm belief from the majority of the departmental team that it provides the best learning environment for the children in the school, mixed ability needs a sustained and practical in-service initiative. The department needs to collaborate, to share in planning of resource material, to talk about strategies and to criticise positively. Of course, there is planning and planning – see figure 11.

Figure 11   Planning for mixed ability

	GOOD INTENTIONS	WHAT REALLY HAPPENED!
September	Head of Departments' meeting. Head launches the idea. DH (Curric.) to set up in-service.	Mutterings of rebellion at the new Head's idea! D.H. Struggling to resolve his disintegrating Timetable. Left a message for the Adviser.
	Head produces paper on mixed ability.	No one reads it – except the Head of English who wrote part of it.
	Departmental meetings to formulate action.	Only the English department responded constructively: all 12 members present at a fiery meeting.
October	Governors informed.	Eyebrows raised . . .
	Conference with staff from schools where mixed ability 'works'.	Industrial Action prevented it.
	Send for stock of early retirement forms.	!
February	Heads of English, Humanities, Science submit new syllabi to DH (Curric).	DH grimaces as they hit his desk, already deep in Headship application forms, room changes and next year's timetable.
March	Rewrite school prospectus and inform parents by letter.	Not done. A full scale 'Inspection' by the Advisory Service is mooted!
April	Order new/extra equipment and materials.	Too late: some didn't arrive in time. Delay worsened by uncertainty about capitation for the coming financial year.
June	Head of Year and DH (C), in consultation with junior schools, draw up mixed ability groups.	Groups in English distorted by decision to form groups on Mathematical ability . . .

The 'good intentions' column is how one school attempted to use available time in order to 'get it right' so far as the children were concerned. The reality can be a lot starker than that. This is the recent experience of one Head of Department:

> It was a new school, operating in purpose-built accommodation, but that's where the advantages seemed to end. Some children were 'creamed off' by a nearby grammar school which took from our catchment area about six or seven of our potential high fliers. They had opened the new school in the first year of ROSLA and had insisted on starting off with five full years, so a reluctant army of disaffected secondary modern kids were forcibly bussed to the new school for an extra year of an education that didn't mean anything to them. It led to a few problems, despite the hard work of the staff. Mixed ability teaching in English was one of the seemingly logical solutions to the predictable troubles the school had had foisted upon it.
>
> ... The catch, of course, was that it wasn't really mixed ability. The department, when I was there, largely failed to grasp the nettle, or seize the opportunity. Admittedly the classes were happier and relationships less tortured, but if you looked through the windows to watch your colleagues teaching (significantly, you wouldn't get through the door!) the style was embarrassingly conventional: desks in rows, teacher at the front reading aloud, or talking, too many glimpses for comfort of *The Art of English*. Because so many of the department were charismatic, experienced or well established the children still benefited, the exam results were acceptable and the parents never questioned the system, but it was, too often for my own peace of mind, a sham.

Why mixed ability teaching in English is an option to be considered

One English Department,[5] committed to the principle of mixed ability to the point where it is practised from first to fifth year inclusive, summarised its reasons for pursuing such a policy in figure 12. Your department might find the accompanying questions a useful basis for discussion.

How does it work in practice?

How far do the suggested activities below, all of which have been used by teachers with mixed ability classes, do what they are designed to do? How would you – and the department in which you work – adapt them? The first two, of course, assume a shared text.

Figure 12   Why mixed ability teaching in English

	Reasons	Questions
1	There is a 'richer' language environment which benefits all pupils.	• Precisely *how* can that richness be achieved?
2	Greater range of experience to be used in discussion and written work.	• How do you encourage the children to respect the experience of others?
3	The students are expected to work to their own potential.	• How can achievement be monitored and recorded?
4	Literature can be enjoyed on various levels.	• What is the place of the class reader?
5	Different assignments can grow out of the same stimulus.	• Who chooses the assignment? What value is there in the principle of 'contract' established between learner and teacher?
6	The same assignment can be done to the level of the individual.	• How do you know what that level is?
7	The variety of activities in English affords the chance of success to all.	• Do all activities in English have equal value?
8	The 'best' teaching style – learning facilitated in individual work or small groups – is encouraged.	• Is there no place left for class teaching in a mixed ability group?
9	Technical skills are *not* best taught to a whole class and emphatically not to a mixed ability class.	• How can individuals be taught necessary 'technical skills'?
10	The fact that the department will share the same problem encourages a sense of teamwork.	• What, in terms of resource making and sharing, can be done to build the sense of corporateness?
11	The 'best' teachers – or the most qualified – do *not* take the 'best' classes.	• How are mixed ability classes drawn up? Randomly? Or with a *genuine* mix? Or by referring to successful teacher/pupil relationships?
12	The sense of failure is lessened.	• How are the gifted to be stretched?
13	There is no sense of inferiority or superiority.	• How do you prevent the children from streaming themselves?
14	How would selection be done anyway?	• What is to be the department's policy on examination entry?
15	The same money is spent on students whatever their ability.	• Shouldn't departmental policy developing year by year allocate extra funds for specific years or problems?

1 FOR A FOURTH-YEAR GROUP

Of Mice and Men
by
John Steinbeck

You should be working in a group of about three people. Choose *two* of
the topics.

1 After discussion and a rough version, devise a well-presented, striking
   WANTED NOTICE issued by the sheriff of Weed for the arrest of
   Lennie and George. Include suitable photographs, *careful* descriptions
   of them, the crime and the reward.

2 Look at chapter 1, particularly pages 1 and 2. Draw a sketch map of
   the area, as if drawn by George for Lennie's benefit. Remember he's
   not terribly bright and needs all the help he can get!

3 Prepare a script for a radio broadcast of chapter 1. It shouldn't last
   longer than three minutes. Tape it! Consider sound effects and
   music.

4 Devise and write a conclusion to the story which involves:

   Slim
   Curley
   Curley's wife
   George and Lennie

---

2 A THIRD-YEAR GROUP

Fireweed
by
Jill Paton Walsh

Do 3 questions in Section A.
Do 2   "   "   "   B.
Do 1   "   "   "   C.

Section A
1 Briefly (no more than six lines) tell the story of the book.
2 Write a sentence about Bill and a sentence about Julie, saying what
   sort of people they are.
3 How do you think you would have got on in a similar situation? Why
   do you think so?
4 What did you think of the book? Which parts did you like best?
5 What do you think happened to Bill in the future?

Section B
1 Find out what you can about what happened in the area where you live during the war.
2 If you liked the book, write a letter to the BBC or ITV suggesting they make a play or film of it. Give some reasons!
3 What's the difference between being 15 or 16 and being 30?
4 Write page 98 (where they sleep together) from *Julie's* point of view.
5 What effect has the war had on Bill? (see page 126 'Not a scratch').

Section C
1 Write a different ending to the story.
2 Write about an experience which meant you had to choose between two people.
3 Write a scene where Bill and Julie meet by accident twenty years later.

3 THIRD-YEAR GROUP: A SHEET DESIGNED TO HELP THE WRITING OF BOOK REVIEWS

1 Give the title, author and publisher of the book.
2 *Briefly* tell the story.

Now choose either Section A or Section B.

Section A
1 Which person in the book did you like most?
2 Draw the cover for the book that you think would be best.
3 What was the most exciting part of the book?
4 Did you enjoy it?
5 Would it make a good TV serial or film?

Section B
1 Who are the most interesting characters in the book? Why?
2 Where is the turning point or climax of the book?
3 What sort of reader is the book aimed at?
4 Is the ending effective?
5 What are the most important themes?

Finally – *for both sections*: write a letter to the author giving your opinion of his/her book and asking some sensible questions.

They worked well within the groups on *Of Mice and Men* – it's a book that always seems to work at any level. It's interesting to reflect that we're using copies passed on to us from the local middle school where it had been banned. Too many 'bastards' in it! The reading was done almost entirely by me, occasionally cutting some of Steinbeck's descriptive writing in the early part of the novel, and with some of the better readers reading the dialogue, playing the role of George, Curley, etc. Typically, I played Lennie throughout!

I don't think I provided enough variety of stimulus in that worksheet – the best work came in the alternative ending section, though the phrasing of that activity isn't very inspiring, is it? There were some good 'Wanted' notices which made for a vivid wall display.

In some ways I preferred the worksheet on *Fireweed*, a novel which, despite its flimsy ending, appealed to that class. I was trying to offer them enough freedom within the structure to be able to respond to the book in a way that was right *for them*. In the event, I renegotiated activities, or at least what I demanded of them.

The sheet aimed at sparking a response from the children about their individual reading is not very successful. I wanted to get away from tired book reviews that painstakingly regurgitated plot, but never expressed an opinion or displayed feelings. Mixed ability teaching should provide an exciting opportunity for departments as a whole to review their policy for building English activities around a novel. If the worksheet isn't the answer, what is?

The examples of work above are all from the same rural comprehensive school: the Head of Department's remarks quoted at the end express the kind of uncertainty that can only be resolved by genuine collaboration within the department.

Examinations, parents, library policy, capitation, liaison – to name but five!

- Who runs the library?

- How much should the department get?

- What kind of liaison should there be between us and the feeder primary schools?

- How can the parents be used and involved?

- What examinations?

'England has no need of a National Lottery; we have O level English Language.'

One way of working
The following is an account by the Head of English at a comprehensive school in the West country showing how he approached the problems listed above. I have inserted material which illustrates or expands on the points made.

Four years into being a Head of an English Department is a good time to take stock. Although, at the outset, I had a 'grand plan', it somehow got lost – submerged in my own version of crisis management, the symptoms of which were a nervous contentment once I was caught up in my teaching, but for the rest of my waking hours manifested themselves in cat-kicking impatience! Then, say eighteen months into the job, I identified things which seemed like priorities: a reform of our policy for examinations; *meaningful* relationships with the primary schools and with parents; a library which got used and a recognition by the Head that our work in the department *was* on the right lines and warranted a major injection of money. Oh yes – and I wanted a major shift in teaching/ learning styles. I set myself two years.

EXAMINATIONS

Circumstances have dictated that examinations have received most attention – things were grindingly average when I arrived: Mode 1 CSE; O Lang. and Lit. and a run-of-the-mill A level course which attracted about ten students a year, most of them girls. Physics often netted upwards of twenty! In some ways I couldn't have chosen a less auspicious time for modification and reform – was someone actually about to announce decisions on 16+? My department, like most others, responded to requests for response to 'national criteria' and the rest, attended meetings, alternately enthused and despaired. Consequently, we have missed the boat on launching a Mode 3. Instead, we have concentrated on switching to the Cambridge Plain Texts paper – an O level Lit. exam which does not stunt enquiry or genuine response. In Literature, above all, the teacher must get out of the way; that is even more the case with examiners. I think it was Raymond O'Malley who, at the inception of the Plain Texts exam, stressed the importance of exams making 'the minimum disturbance to good teaching'. The students are allowed copies of studied texts into the exam with them and the questions ask for personal opinion and for response on the lines of 'Imagine you were a character'. The questions *create* knowledge, rather than just test it:

Read the following poem carefully a number of times. It was written about 140 years ago, and concerns a simpler world where a journey might be made by a small boat and on foot. (Perhaps the boat is a canoe? Perhaps the farm is on an island?) The poem concerns the sensations of a man journeying to meet his lover, and their meeting.

Write about the poem, saying whether you agree with me that the words chosen by the poet, and the way he uses them, make the sensations vivid and urgent to a reader. Would you say that it is an interesting poem? Try to explain your answer – but keep to the poem as a poem.

Meeting at Night

The grey sea and the long black land;
And the yellow half-moon large and low;
And the startled little waves that leap
In fiery ringlets from their sleep,
As I gain the cove with pushing prow,
And quench its speed i' the slushy sand.

> Then a mile of warm sea-scented beach;
> Three fields to cross till a farm appears;
> A tap at the pane, the quick sharp scratch
> And blue spurt of a lighted match,
> And a voice less loud, through its joys and fears,
> Than the two hearts beating each to each!
>
> Robert Browning

One of the unexpected benefits is the effect the [Cambridge Plain Texts] paper has had on approaches to literature and teaching/learning styles down through the school. The next phase is to shift our A level to one that is compatible with the Plain Texts. That we have not yet done so is because we cannot decide where to jump. The department is attracted to working within a consortium, or opting for AEB syllabus 753, or even looking closely at Communication Studies. We must make a decision soon – and note the democratic tone!

Of course the biggest challenges are to come: 16+ is now with us and, presumably, my kids will be sitting the first GCSE exams in the summer of 1988. But will they be sitting the same paper? Will it be just the top 60 per cent? And will the best elements of the current system – teacher involvement, course work, talk, etc. – be retained?

There are two useful NATE publications on examinations:

- *Alternatives at English A level.*
- *English: Teachers and the Examination Boards.*

SPELLING

And then we got bogged down in the spelling controversy. Imagine the scene: third year Parents' Evening – late – the hour when your eyes blur and the mind reels with politeness. You'd even prefer to be marking! Stroppy parent criticises junior member of staff about his total inability to teach spelling. Worse – he can't even spell himself . . . What do I propose to do about it? Good question. What do I tackle first: the teacher who can't or the policy which isn't?

How long have you been writing for? I wouldn't mind been a writer but I'm not all that good at spelling as you might find out as you read my letter.

From a letter to Gene Kemp by Sharon Carver of Leeds.

Herd the one About . . .
Brian Patten has just been sent a CSE English exam paper that contains an embarrassing question about one of his own poems. 'Why,' it asks, 'has the poet misspelt "heard" in this extract?'

The poem was called 'Little Johnny's Final Letter' and the line ran: 'Herd your poem on the radio this morning.' The examiners obviously hoped that pupils would grapple with emergent pretension and see the inherent pun which locates, with a hint at illiteracy, the intrinsic herd element that underlies the very act of mass media listenership. Unfortunately, that isn't why Patten wrote it.

'I'm just a rotten speller.' he explained last week. 'I thought that was how you were supposed to spell it. My publishers usually spot my mistakes, but they missed that one. God knows what those kids wrote about in the exam.'

From the *Guardian*

The issue wouldn't lie down – the Head complained bitterly to me about the standard of report writing from some members of the department. Reports were returned by Heads of House with incorrect spellings ringed: it all created a lot of bad feeling, but at least it made us talk the issue through. What *did* we all do to improve the spelling and the grasp of the other conventions of written English for our pupils? We studied the writing of some of our children over a period of time – and recognised that our attempts to foster basic writing skills were haphazard, sometimes left to mere chance. We established a system to tackle the problem head on:

- We should attempt to agree about what really matters amongst ourselves.

- We should ensure that redrafting was a normal part of the writing process for our children and, consequently, we, as well as the children, should be involved in questioning the effectiveness, appropriateness and accuracy of what was in the throes of being written. We avoided the 'teacher as examiner' mode as much as possible.

- We endeavoured to deal with problems on an individual basis, and to get the children both interested in words and sensitive to their own weaknesses and strengths.

- We outlawed all spelling tests *except* those which tested the individual child's vocabulary: students kept personal dictionaries of their own words, either words incorrectly spelled during written assignments, or words on topics that interested them.

- We all concentrated on the 'Look, Cover, Write, Check' model for spelling:

Look: pupil looks at the word until its visual image is 'caught'.
Cover: pupil covers the word up.
Write: pupil writes the word as quickly as possible, without interruption if possible and in a flowing style of handwriting.
Check: he or she checks their version against the original.

CAPITATION

My Head does not believe in open government: no one knows officially who is on what scale, or the reason, and capitation is kept as a closely guarded secret, known only to the Head's secretary – or so it seems sometimes. We make bids for money and, sometimes as late as a month into the new financial year, we receive a sealed envelope with a printed slip inside indicating the departmental allowance.

Take this year: I have just been promised £2,000 to spend and when it comes I will be tempted to jump for joy and fantasise of doing something innovative in the subject. The urge will soon fade for the £2000 that to me is a dream holiday in the Bahamas is, in the terms of the English stock cupboards, a wet weekend in Bournemouth. The money soon goes.

The terrible conclusion is that my £2,000, about par for the course these days, means that I have, in toto, £2.22 per pupil per year to educate that child in its mother tongue and literary heritage. With any amount of efficiency and dedicated teaching, it simply cannot be done.

Martin Booth writing in the *Guardian* (1984)

Martin Booth's £2.22 per pupil may even be better than average. Capitation can often bring on an attack of unexpected coyness from teachers comparing notes. Heads of English may feel that revealing their own departmental allowance can inadvertently identify their personal standing within the school in which they teach. Heads, as a rule, don't pour good money after bad. However, these figures (at July 1984) give an interesting view of the spread across the country as a whole:

	Pupils	Budget	Comments
School 1	900	£2,000	Includes stationery.
" 2	1,100	£2,100	Includes stationery (13–18).
" 3	1,100	£1,700	Library separate (11–16).
" 4	?	?	Member of dept. uncertain: about £1.50 per pupil?
" 5	1,400	£3,000+	
" 6	1,500	£2,300–£2,500	
" 7	1,100	£2,300	There is an equation system for allocating money (11–18).
" 8	1,100	£1,800	Teacher not certain.

Such a very random sample, with an approximate expenditure of £1.88 per pupil, tells us little except to reinforce the need for more openness in dealing with the matter, from English teacher to English teacher on the one hand, and between Heads and Heads of Department on the other.

What have I done to attract more money in our direction? Well, for a start I've got the Head working in the department. He teaches one fourth-year CSE group and he regularly attends departmental meetings. The department has embarked upon a number of projects which have cross-curricular implications. We are involved in some work with the Computer Studies department, for example, and are pressing hard for extra money to fund these. Finally, we have increased the visibility of the department, both around the school and in terms of extra-curricular activities: our display is more effective; the bookshop is open more often; there are more school productions with deliberately larger casts; the school magazine still appears, but the lower school now produces a newspaper once a month; we have more frequent theatre trips, for staff as well as kids; we are in there fighting for pupils at the point when they are due to opt for sixth-form courses.

Bound up with activities like these is a much more systematic approach to delegation and therefore job descriptions. *Every* member of department has a job description which has been mutually negotiated and agreed. Of equal importance is the fact that responsibilities within the department are changed regularly, so that members of the team feel that their own professional expertise is being extended.

THE LIBRARY

First of all, the *good* features:

- it is open every day before school, after school and during the lunch hour;

- it is widely used, by staff as well;

- it is *not* used as a teaching space during the day;

- the pupils are involved in its running;

- it is centrally situated and attractively appointed;

But we still need to:

- agree a library policy to support the whole school curriculum;

- get parents involved;

- link the bookshop and the library more effectively;

- have a proper selection policy;

- increase our paperback fiction;

- extend our non-book resources;

- withdraw outdated stock;

- publicise the library more effectively;

- (most important of all) negotiate a proper arrangement for control of the library: appoint someone as Librarian who has a real knowledge of children's books – and a passion for it; ensure that the Librarian has sufficient time and backing to do a worthwhile job.

LIAISON

For the most part our meetings were rather lacklustre affairs until we chanced on an obvious way forward: we worked jointly on a project. In producing a collection of writing from the family of schools, we forgot about earlier doubts and reservations and began to collaborate ...

The recently published (1983) *Language Across the Transition*[6] made a number of positive recommendations about the transfer of pupils and liaison between schools. In summary, these are:

1   *Meetings*: between teachers with a common subject interest to plan for continuity – for clearly defined purposes.
2   *Visits*: for children; for staff; and for parents.
3   *Exchanges*: teachers switch schools for a limited period of time.
4   *Projects*:

- publish an anthology from the family of schools;

- publish pamphlets about English as it is taught in the secondary school;

- study together the development of children's language (particular individuals);

- children work on two-term projects bridging the point of transfer.

5   *Negotiations*: about what is handed over when the children move on.

AND PARENTS?

Use, inform, involve them in every way possible.

- Teach parents in with the children if the opportunity arises.

- Get parents in to talk about life, work, memories, skills.

- Show parents work in drama, writing, etc. Make them a real and valued audience.

- Discuss books with parents, perhaps at informal evening meetings.

- Sell parents books from the school bookshop.

- Encourage parents' participation in school theatre trips, etc.

- Show parents why you've made decisions.

- 'Know' parents – know what expertise is available.

- Make parents feel welcome in school.

- Ensure that any system of communication is *genuinely* open to a two-way flow.

5   Evaluation

I spent six hours in the store cupboard sorting *masses* of totally redundant stock. The survey had rendered useless, at a stroke, 90 per cent of language resource material.

I find most teachers of English set out only to correct simple mistakes. From past experience I have seen that *they don't get involved enough* in the reading of the work which might have taken a couple hours to do. They go through the work like demented robots.[1]

'Evaluation' is a word that threatens. It implies that it is someone's intention to evaluate *you*; it has connotations of inspection and surveillance. One teacher friend of mine overcame this difficulty when I was involved in an 'inspection' of his school. 'That gentleman I told you about has come today,' he said to his first-year drama group. 'Kids, here [pointing to me] is my grandad!'

In reality, evaluation is inextricably bound up with the fundamentals of teaching English. It formalises the process of monitoring the pupils' development and the situations and structures in which they learn most effectively, Equally, it necessitates fostering an awareness of our own strengths and weaknesses and those of the department as a whole. The two observations quoted at the outset of this chapter indicate the extent to which honest criticism can affect both teaching and learning. The first comment is that of a Head of Department who has just spearheaded a *collaborative* review of the department's resources for 'language work'; the acid remarks about marking are those of a fourth-year pupil. We can learn from *both* parties engaged in teaching and learning, and the perceptions of those involved in the classroom activity are likely to be more sharp-edged and realistic than those of outsiders. Self-criticism is already part-way towards a shift in technique or policy. Where the outsider can serve a useful function is in raising questions or providing a mirror in which it is easier to identify a clear image.

Although the pattern in Figure 13 seems predictable, there are some important underlying questions:

Figure 13

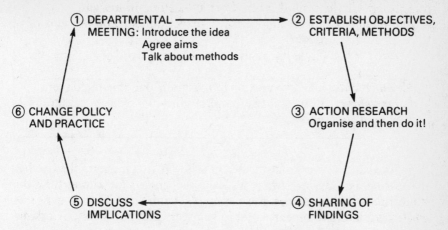

- *Who* decides what we want to know? If the decision is perceived as initiating from the Headteacher, senior management, or even the Head of Department, it may not touch the hearts and minds of the individual department members – let alone their classrooms!

- How do you avoid negative criticism? People change only if they want to.

- Can a department be *too* collaborative? One teacher identified a potential problem thus: 'Where analysis produces paralysis, someone has to say what must be done.'

- Is too much navel-contemplation just another form of self-abuse? Is there a danger that we can become *too* preoccupied with the same predictable issues?

Marking policy

During one week several summers ago, I estimated that I had 'marked' some 67,000 words of children's writing: the length of a short novel. To many teachers, marking can become a treadmill. English teachers in particular feel under constant pressure from the sheer weight of varied writing that comes their way. I know of only one school where the Head (himself an ex-Head of English) has given his teachers of English less pupil-contact time in an attempt to compensate for the marking load.

In such circumstances it is not surprising if policies for marking sometimes lack clarity; too much contact with a red biro numbs the mind! Above all else, the kind of response from the teacher should be appropriate to the type of writing. A marking policy which is not flexible is therefore a straitjacket restraining both teacher and child, for example:

Spelling: Circle around error. Correct spelling in margin.
Punctuation: Circle around error. Correct punctuation at point of
  error; P in margin.
Incorrect word: Cross through error. Correct word if possible, in
  margin.
Meaning unclear: '?' by error or in margin if one line or longer.
Paragraphing: Two oblique parallel lines // where paragraph
  should have ended.

A policy that sets out ground rules in this way is cementing the teacher
into a role as examiner when we have recognised for a long time the
value of varied audiences for children's writing: child to teacher as
trusted adult, child to peer, child to younger child and so on. 'Marking'
is more than proof reading.

In providing the agenda for discussion in figure 14, I have juxtaposed
one department's self-questioning on marking with a collection of
comments from children about *their* response to the way their work is
treated. Interestingly and significantly, the two sets of comments/
questions are separated by several years and nearly 100 miles.

The pupils' comments in figure 14 provide a framework within which
we can more easily clarify departmental policy. They have much to
contribute in terms of knowing what 'works' best for them and, typically,
in their transparent honesty when genuinely involved in what they are
doing. This honesty is manifested disarmingly when the children are
invited to contribute to the assessment of their performance during a
term – writing their own reports, for example – or, as suggested in item
6 of figure 14:

Teacher: Very, very disappointing, Paul. This would have no
             value at all if anyone was to find it in a hundred years.
             Much more detail is needed. What's wrong with your
             English at the moment?

Pupil: I agree, Miss Cameron. My homework has been bad
             lately so I will try to make an improvement with my
             work by spending half an hour on it.

Teacher: Good – lively conversation, but could you have said
             any more?

Pupil: I think if I had tried I could have said more but I was
             working in a group that was miles away from each other
             and we couldn't work together.

Figure 14   Marking

The teacher ←————————————————————→ The pupils

	The teacher	The pupils
1	When you are marking, are you conscious of the difference between response, assessment and correction?	'I think that a teacher's comments should concentrate less on technical merit. They should be used to inspire you and reflect the effort put into the piece.'
2	Are proof reading and correction a significant teaching strategy?	'If you do spellings wrong I think they should be corrected and spelt right because you could then learn how to spell the words correctly.'
3	Do you mark in the presence of the pupil–writer?	'The work should be marked in front of the person concerned. It may help them to understand where they are going wrong. Also you can talk to the teacher about the work.'
4	Is your comment a genuine part of the dialogue between teacher and pupil?	'I like the comments to encourage me and also to point out any faults. I think it needs to be a personal comment just as if the teacher was speaking instead of writing.'
5	Do you grade or put a written comment, or both?	'I think my work is marked to give me an idea of the standard of my work. Also marking creates a competitive situation which can push some people to better work. (I don't consider this works for everyone).'
6	How can we get the children more involved in the process?	'We should be allowed to put answers to teachers' comments such as, "I know this was not my best work. I will do better in future."'
7	How does 'marking' relate to redrafting?	'If a piece of work is put on the wall you don't want red circles and lines all over it. The teacher should just tell the person who did it what the mistakes are.'
8	Are you sensitive enough to the children's anxiety about marking?	'I don't like it when you have to call your mark out. Especially when it's bad.'
9	Are you the only audience for the writing?	'I like it when we read each other's work, especially when it's stories or poems. We can usually tell what's good and bad about them, although I think the teacher should mark them as well'
10	What value is there in the pupils marking each other's work?	'I think we should be able to mark our own work once in a while and then talk about it with the teacher'

Some departments have made a point of investigating the children's perceptions on the marking of their work. The responses certainly raise some doubts:

- 'Do you look at spelling corrections?' (*Always* – 15; *sometimes* – 11; *never* – 0.)

- 'If a spelling is corrected for you, do you remember it?' (*Always* – 4; *sometimes* – 22; *never* – 0.)

- 'Do you take more notice of corrections if your book is given back quickly?' (*Yes* – 8; *no* – 10; *don't mind* – 8.)

'Asking the kids' will produce gems of inescapable logic:'Teachers should spend longer marking our work. They should spend at least five minutes on each story or piece of work. They should be paid more money for this'!

Focusing on talk

One of the major benefits of a sustained evaluation exercise is that it brings an issue clearly to the fore. This is especially valuable if the department has determined on a policy of evaluating the kind and quality of discussion work in English classrooms. For one thing, it ensures that, because it is on the agenda, more of 'it' happens. More importantly, it accords it a status which it might otherwise have lacked, both with the staff and children. Talking about talk – and; better still, engaging in attempts to judge its quality and plan for its improvement – raises it to where it belongs, at the forefront of our work.

Case study: an English department troubled about talking
An HMI had triggered the doubts off. In an after-school comment to Mark Smith, the Head of English, she had confided about another unnamed school which she had recently visited: 'It was entirely teacher-centred. There wasn't one occasion when any one child was encouraged to talk to another.' Mark had smiled and wondered how much genuine pupil/pupil talk his department had exposed to the HMI during the day. He had a feeling he knew!

Phase 1: What we wanted to do
One of my principal difficulties is running the department has always been the breadth of experience and philosophy that exists amongst us – we're all so different. We mean such different things on occasions when, initially, we seemed in agreement. I know that the *experience* of English a child will get at this school is very much a matter of luck; it shouldn't be, but how do you evolve a consensus approach with staff as varied as Sybil (55, scale 2 since 1969, responsibility for CSE, member of the Professional Association of Teachers, appointed by my predecessor

thrice removed!) and Chris (25, second year of teaching, ex-lorry driver and bass guitarist with Electric Snake)? It's a wonder that we talk at all, let alone the kids . . .

We spent a tense half-hour at a departmental meeting when Barbara (second in department) reported back on a course she had attended about 'Evaluation'. Our intention – Barbara and I – was to railroad the rest of the team into a collaborative investigation into the kind of 'pupil talk' that's going on in our classrooms. First problem: Sybil questions the whole principle of encouraging talk – 'They just gossip if you let them' – and we sit and suffer! Piqued by our failure to respond, she lapses into a menopausal sulk. I made a mental note to manipulate a situation where she and Chris can work together on something; surprisingly, she'll take things from him she wouldn't from anyone else.

The meeting improved after that: we talked ourselves past cynicism and even suspicion. We agreed *what* we should focus on – the effectiveness of our small group discussion work; *how* we should conduct the investigation – tape-recordings plus transcriptions, questionnaires for the kids, looking at written drafts before and after structured small group work, passive outside observer; and *why* we were doing it – for us and therefore the kids themselves, and not for the senior management (one of whom teaches English!).

Figure 15

Topic/area for investigation	How it was done	Comment
1 Quantity of small group work: how much really goes on?	(i) Questionnaire for all members of dept.	The range was wide as expected though we all claim to do it.
	(ii) And for two samples from years 1 to 4.	Some classes say they NEVER experience group work in English (see above!)
	(iii) Questionnaire to selected other depts. for comment.	Raises some interesting points about our (stillborn) language policy.
2 Areas of English work where pupil/pupil talk seems most appropriate.	Each pair chose specific areas to investigate, e.g. poetry, writing, problem-solving, and reported back at a series of dept. meetings using selected transcription.	Served to highlight those parts of our empire where talk seldom reaches! Exam. classes at 5th year level especially.
3 Size of groups: what's the best number?	Comparison by pairs of teachers: one evaluating the same task set by the other teacher to groups of different sizes.	Much of our work seems best suited to groups of 3 or 4. A pair is usually more purposeful than, say, 6 or 7.
4 The teacher's role in group work?	Comparison of taped discussion with and without teacher involvement.	The discussions are *very* different!
5 Composition of groups?	One teacher in the pair always allowed friendship groupings; the other, with the same task, insisted on his/her grouping. Comparison of resulting work.	A lot of argument on this one: we couldn't agree!

Phase 2: What we discovered
We worked in pairs, taking a particular area for investigation each. This seemed to reduce the sense of threat and helped sustain what turned out to be an extended piece of work. I've summarised the findings in figure 15.

Phase 3: Where do we go from here?

So where *does* Mark's department go next? (See figure 16.)

Figure 16   Policy development

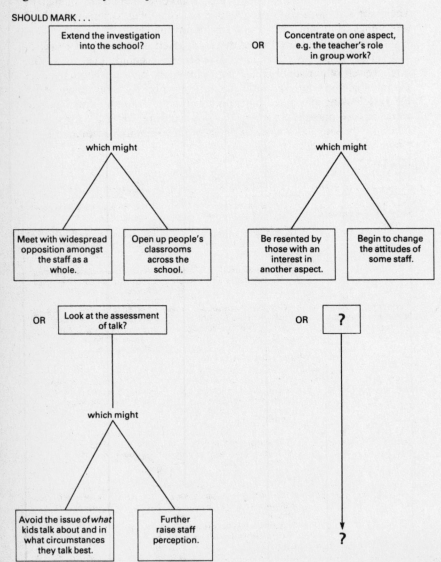

Continuing, classroom-based evaluation

Close, objective scrutiny of the department's practice once begun can never end. It goes far beyond nebulous discussion about aims and objectives[2] – and obviously so, because it is classroom-based and to do with the experience of English any child will get as they pass through the school. It should lead to greater coherence of policy and a more certain sense of purpose, not least because of the inevitable, perhaps unconscious, move towards collaboration amongst the departmental team. It isn't good enough really to accept a multi-headed English curriculum and to expect the children to make sense of a subject that appears to shift its ground from classroom to classroom. The children themselves have much to contribute:[3] they can focus the mind wonderfully. One 8–12 middle school had set out on an investigation into the factors affecting their children's reading success:

> None could remember first liking books – 'always' seemed the general opinion. They read widely, mainly fiction, some poetry, some non-fiction for general interest, or to follow up a special hobby. Choice was guided by book cover, size of print, chapters (considered 'a good thing') and what was being read aloud in class. Sometimes they choose an author they had read before. They did not often re-read, just sometimes going back to favourite stories or parts of books. They all belonged to the public library and had many books at home.

With that picture of what constitutes success, it is easier for a department to plan accordingly. Acting on a hunch – or worse, a bunch of hunches – cannot but be random and potentially superficial or irrelevant.

Profiling
'Accountability' is rapidly and tediously becoming a 1980s vogue word. Like much educational jargon it means different things to different people and was, no doubt, conceived in some scurvy politician's grand design. In the classroom, teachers are accountable to the children. The English teacher should feel a deep obligation to help each child to an understanding, an awareness and an appreciation of language. The department as a team should evolve policy that ensures that nothing intrudes between the learner and the teacher. Profiling, for example, should not be a side of A4 drawn up by a working party and accepted without question by the department; all too easily it can become a fatuous checklist attempting to monitor, in isolation, skills that are inextricably threaded together:

English Department Checklist

Please indicate in the first box when the point has been covered. Subsequent revision lessons should be indicated in the remaining boxes. Ensure that, whenever possible, all points have been covered during the course of the school year. Additional points should be added in the spaces provided:

Year 1 Language   Literature

Sentence – simple			
Full stop			
Comma			
Phrase			
Noun			
Verb			
Adjective			
Speech mark			
Spelling rules (1–10)			
SRA Reading Lab.			
Exclamation mark			
Question mark			

Narrative sequence			
Hero			
Villain			
Characterisation (simple)			
Climax			
Dialogue			
Rhyme (simple)			
Rhythm (simple)			
Simile			

Equally, the profile can reduce the child's achievement to a meaningless list of grades or ticks, as in figure 17.

Figure 17

	WRITING				TALKING				READING			COMMENTS
Wayne Williams	C	C	B	C–	D	C	C–	D	D+	D		Worse than his brother!
	Spelling	Punctuation	Creativity	Style	In groups	In class	Clarity of argument	Vocabulary	Comprehension	Reading aloud		

In constructing pupil profiles, the *purpose* of the activity should not be lost sight of. It is an attempt to monitor development, diagnose weakness, exploit strength, and a means whereby the child can get to know himself or herself more thoroughly. It follows therefore that the child should be involved in the process.

GUIDELINES ON PROFILES

- Is the assessment of the pupil's work negotiated with the pupil?

- If test scores are used, it is clear *what* was tested and why? Are the scores regarded with due suspicion?

- Does the profile include useful information – it should all be useful! – like a record of the child's reading tastes, or examples at different stages of his or her writing?

- Is the profile easily accessible?

- Is the profile not too demanding in terms of the amount of time it takes to complete?

- Does the profile in its categorisation of the aspects of language bear genuine relation to the realities of what happens in the school's English classrooms?

- Does the form to be filled in go beyond ticking boxes?[4]

The price of rigid thinking

All the indications are that over-formal assessment procedures are likely, in their mechanistic way, to gnaw at the edges – or even the heart – of what we hold to be English. Tests are usually designed to expose failure. Graded tests are not an answer either; an argument in their favour was set out in an article by Bob Moon in *The Times Educational Supplement*[5] when he fantasised about a school where graded tests held sway:

> The school no longer takes subject O levels in English Language or the arts. Each of the four has covered a programme leading to graded tests assessing a basic level of written and spoken communication. Paul has already acquired the top level, Jenny, level one, and Stephen and Louise are debating whether to attempt the one from the top. Paul has begun a Mode 3 O level-type literature which takes him away from the group.

There is, perhaps, a superficial attraction to such a scenario, but it ignores many important points:

- Where does the literature go?

- What are the effects on the curriculum? Won't the test wag the dog?

- What happens when it becomes apparent that some children may not get beyond 'level one'? What happens to motivation then?

- The effect on teaching/learning relationships and styles. The likelihood is that those styles most common in the teaching for the more conventional examinations at 16+ will become the norm across the whole school.

It does not need assessment which is either graded or, in the conventional sense, tested to enable us to report on what students achieve if our primary concern is that the student should get a sense of coherence and purpose. Such ends can be achieved by involving students in assessing their own progress and by discussing the long term, as well as the short-term aims of the subject with them.[6]

Finally . . .

'And what is the examiner supposed to make of this, then, Saville? "Discuss the imagery of the poem below", and all I can find on your paper is a turgid, unrhythmical and, if I may say so, singularly inept poem of your own construction . . . Wordsworth wrote poetry and if he, in some idle moment, and on the margin of his examination paper, had given me his rendering of "I wandered lonely as a cloud", I wouldn't, I venture to suggest, have been altogether displeased. Provided he had kept it to the margin; and providing that he'd answered the question put to him in full.'[7]

6 Micros and English

For most teachers of English there are two very different kinds of computer program. Both of them, in different ways, chill the soul: turgid drill and practice (cynical kids obediently jumping through hoops), and the more insidious video game that serves to numb the brain. Joseph Weizenbaum, writing in the *Guardian*[1] and from his position as Professor of Computer Science at the Massachusetts Institute of Technology, put it like this:

> There is an eager market in this world for people who are already psychically numb by the time they enter the world's workforces, that is, who are superbly trained to make no connections between what they do and the ultimate effect of what they do on what might be called the end users of the product of their labours.
>
> Most of the computer and arcade games I have seen are trainers for just that skill. Spaceships and airplanes are shot down in great numbers. Megaton bombs shower whole countries. Many games are so constructed that there can be no survivors . . . There is even a computer game on the American market called 'Custer's Revenge' in which that player wins who has raped the most American Indian women. In that game, the most gruesome and frightful insult a man can wreak upon a woman is cleansed of all torment, horror, anguish. Only abstract operations on plastic buttons remain. This is what I mean by psychic numbing.

So why bother?

There will be those who say that an English department of the mid and late 1980s which has not fully considered the use and potential of the microcomputer will increasingly be guilty of unthinking conservatism. The much misunderstood Ned Ludd's name usually crops up here. Without doubt, though, such a department will have failed the pupils, leaving them with a message, unspoken but firmly spelt out, that computers are for maths and science – oh yes, and for the real world where the wonders of micro-technology are nonchalantly accepted as commonplace.

The financial argument – 'Where's the money coming from, then?' –

will soon wither. We have already reached that point in time when an English department can purchase the cheapest home computer on the market for less than a set of thirty books; it is clearly also time that teachers of English confronted the microtech revolution and established a realistic, meaningful departmental policy towards it.

'Computer' is an unfortunate word. For years many of us were content to believe that a computer's sole function was computation, that those thin sheets of printout were patterned with nothing more than tedious figures. But, incontestably, computers are sophisticated and flexible users of language. 'Yes,' people say, but what does the computer do that you can't do with books, paper, chalk and talk?' It's a valid question that demands a considered answer: after all, money spent on software is money not spent on books. Clearly, there should be more to the enterprise than merely raising students' consciousness about the likely impact of computer technology. English teachers, while recognising that they do have a role to play in establishing computer literacy, should be concerned above all to make full use of the technology, augmenting and extending English work by exploiting its potential: as a writing instrument, as a framework for talk and as a highly sophisticated information storage and retrieval system. In time, the microcomputer will prove at least as useful an adjunct in the English teacher's classroom as a television, video or tape-recorder. With imaginative software it can motivate students very powerfully; respond to instructions at phenomenal speed; lead students unsuspectingly into genuine considerations of language use; radically alter the nature of the writing process and free the teacher to participate in the lesson, rather than over-direct it.

Unnervingly, the children are likely to be more confident with the hardware than we are. Many adults suffer from 'technofear', that feeling triggered off in the past by language labs, tape-recorders and video machines. There can't be many more confidence-shaking moments for a teacher under the unsympathetic scrutiny of thirty pairs of eyes than when the tape breaks or the new video recorder refuses to respond like its predecessor to tentative handling. Micros are probably even more likely to make your fingers shake, at least on first acquaintance; this state of affairs will not – cannot – last for ever:

> The mystique must go and the machinery accorded as much or as little respect as a typewriter, tape-recorder or television set. Typically, the children have adapted more quickly than we have: they are more at ease and accept the micro-revolution without so much as a flicker of doubt.[2]

We do, however, have a right to be uneasy. The revolution has been so rapid for one thing, catching most of us unawares: 'If the auto industry had done what the computer industry has done in the last 30 years, a Rolls-Royce would cost $2.50 and get 2,000,000 miles to the gallon.'[3]

Departments wishing to assess the computer's potential within the language environment they are trying to establish would do well initially to organise a meeting in which they *participate* – in the role of learners – in a simulation-style computer program. This could be done within the English Department, or perhaps in conjunction with teachers of English from neighbouring schools, or perhaps Humanities teachers from the same school. It is really only through participation that the value of the microcomputer, as a means whereby purposeful discussion can be stimulated in the classroom, can be fully appreciated. The kind of small group discussion produced is vibrant and alive; in the end it *matters* what decisions are made. Good English-teaching practice for many years has involved structuring group-talking activities in such a way that concepts are clarified, emotions explored, prejudice exposed, mutual decisions reached. Talk as a means of learning is at its most efficacious when it is tentative, when it builds on previously debated theories and attitudes, and when people listen to each other within the group because they want to and they think it necessary.

Case study: 'Space Programme Alpha'
'Tuesday morning at Altwood School in Maidenhead. Class 3Y is some weeks into 'Space Programme Alpha'; it is the first time they have seen a microcomputer in an English classroom. The teacher, Joan Ashton, describes the activity: 'It includes a computer program,[4] an assignment manual and other written material and the whole package is intended to develop the full range of English skills.'

Used to working in groups, the children are well aware of what is expected of them. Three of the groups are engaged at various points along the simulation, sitting around tables in a classroom where the walls are covered with maps, drawings and a range of writing related to the simulated space mission. The fourth group is alone in the stock cupboard with the computer, responding to the program and recording their reactions in the 'Captain's log' – a cassette recorder which will be the focus of the group's follow-up once the program itself has been completed. The teacher's comments on class 3Y are relevant here: . . . 'their previous teacher had expressed concern over the general lack of motivation and effort. After a few weeks of teaching them before this activity, I also felt concerned about this.'

As part of the evaluation process, an outside observer made the following written comments during the lesson:

A group of seven (too large?) in front of the VDU. A disappointingly fuzzy picture. The four girls and three boys are very enthusiastic, almost ignoring me as an outsider. The talk, however, seems – at this stage at least – to be very hectic and there's not much real listening going on . . . Once they've started determining roles, it would be interesting to see them being encouraged through drama to confirm those roles. The instructions sometimes lack clarity, both in terms of the use of colour and through misuse of language. It's impressive how the children become very good at listening once there is a *real* problem to solve.

In evaluating software, it helps to look at the activity through the children's eyes, recognising that their perceptions can differ greatly from the teacher's and that such insights matter. Fifth-year computer students at the same Maidenhead school, were asked to comment on 'Space Programme Alpha' with regard to 'program design': screen displays, memory use, by-passes to avoid complex or long-winded instructions/procedures. The groups who used the program as part of their English work commented usefully afterwards on several aspects of it: the sounds, graphics, the degree of user-friendliness the need for the teacher as an additional helper, the parts they particularly liked or disliked. Their response was detailed and enthusiastic:

'It brought us together in groups and in doing so made us work as a whole instead of an individual which is much more enjoyable.'

'It gave us a special sense of responsibility.'

'You learn more by talking about things.'

'We enjoyed the responsibility of making decisions.'

Sally is a member of class 3Y. She is writing an account of the mission with the benefit of the tape-recorded 'captain's log'; her involvement is reassuring, evident and highly individual:

> *Sally*: Everything was fine until something disturbed the ship's navigational system. This is my fault – without electronic aids I get lost very easily . . . everyone blamed me and shouted and hurled insults and saying I should have done this and that and not what I did do. Now – orders and people who think they know better than me is one thing I can't stand.

The syntax of that final sentence hints at one of the great strengths of the activity: Sally is in role. Having experienced the situation, she is able to write about it forcefully and perceptively.

The evidence is that children whose teachers are using micros as part of their English find it absorbing and highly motivating. It would be perverse to ignore the potential of a resource which may well – given development of the right sort of software – be liberating for teachers and pupils alike.

A solution in search of a problem?

Figure 18 could provide the basis for a departmental meeting. There is a short section on implications, an attempt to sketch current developments and potential and the final section is an invitation to negotiate the department's chosen criteria for buying software. It is suggested at the end of figure 18 you complete the phrase 'a program should . . .', considering both the criteria already identified in the figure and other criteria which you feel have been omitted.

Figure 18   Micros and English; software; a program should . . .

1 Uses

Type	Benefits	Comments
1 Simulation and adventure games	• A framework for purposeful talk. • Use of the micro here offers speed of response, graphics and sound. • A creative and imaginative option. • Works well in a mixed ability context. • Can fit neatly into 'English' activities. • Incorporates decision making, problem solving; can include role play, code breaking, 'language' activities, etc.	• Commercial adventure games can be excessively competitive. • Potential for self-generated adventure games, with the children in charge. • Some games are based around fiction, e.g. *The Hobbit* and *Nineteen Eighty-Four*. • 'Educational' simulation usually involves extensive courseware. • Without courseware, the program itself can be restricted by its limited vocabulary.
2 Word processing	• Redrafting: 'automatic Tipp-Ex'. It allows the movement of whole paragraphs; insertion/deletion of individual words or whole sentences.	• 'With the computer as a writing instrument . . . students . . . can gain the immediate and personal satisfaction of seeing their work as they would like it to be presented – Anthony Adams. • The micro-writer . . . a hand-held word processor.
3 'Word–crafting'	• Allows children to experiment with words, shape, colour and movement in writing poetry.	• By using computers creatively and collaboratively, children can create 'poetry like living sculpture' – Frank Smith. • Examples include 'ADD–VERSE' and 'WORD–DANCE'.
4 Language–focused	• Group work can get children actively involved in 'joint linguistic experiments'! • A 'construction kit for language' (Mike Sharples). • Branching 'story-makers' where the children can choose the further development of a story.	• Avoid 'Electronic Ridout'. • 'A set of tools to explore, construct and modify text; a stock-pile of useful linguistic parts such as definitions and synonyms, a detailed instruction manual describing the function of each tool and a "Teach Yourself" guide suggesting games, exercises and projects in story building' – (based on *Language in Use*.)
5 Information storage and retrieval	• Pupils can devise their own data files for *real* purposes. • An important area for developing the skills of 'interrogating a data base', finding things out: 'asking questions getting answers'.	• See Patrick Scott's article in *Exploring English With Microcomputers*, CET (1983). • 'If pupils are to acquire the skills they will need for access to and control over information sources, then they will need to learn: (i) How to create their own files; (ii) How to use their files to answer their own questions – *Teaching Humanities in the Microelectronic Age*, Adams and Jones (1983).

Continued on page 96

Figure 18 Continued from page 95

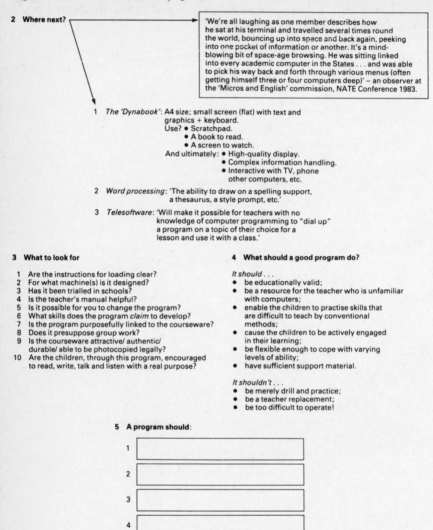

2 Where next?

'We're all laughing as one member describes how
he sat at his terminal and travelled several times round
the world, bouncing up into space and back again, peeking
into one pocket of information or another. It's a mind-
blowing bit of space-age browsing. He was sitting linked
into every academic computer in the States . . . and was able
to pick his way back and forth through various menus (often
getting himself three or four computers deep)' – an observer at
the 'Micros and English' commission, NATE Conference 1983.

1 *The 'Dynabook'*: A4 size; small screen (flat) with text and
     graphics + keyboard.
     Use? ● Scratchpad.
         ● A book to read.
         ● A screen to watch.
     And ultimately: ● High-quality display.
           ● Complex information handling.
           ● Interactive with TV, phone
            other computers, etc.

2 *Word processing*: 'The ability to draw on a spelling support,
     a thesaurus, a style prompt, etc.'

3 *Telesoftware*: 'Will make it possible for teachers with no
     knowledge of computer programming to "dial up"
     a program on a topic of their choice for a
     lesson and use it with a class.'

3 What to look for

1 Are the instructions for loading clear?
2 For what machine(s) is it designed?
3 Has it been trialled in schools?
4 Is the teacher's manual helpful?
5 Is it possible for you to change the program?
6 What skills does the program *claim* to develop?
7 Is the program purposefully linked to the courseware?
8 Does it presuppose group work?
9 Is the courseware attractive/ authentic/
    durable/ able to be photocopied legally?
10 Are the children, through this program, encouraged
    to read, write, talk and listen with a real purpose?

4 What should a good program do?

It should . . .
● be educationally valid;
● be a resource for the teacher who is unfamiliar
  with computers;
● enable the children to practise skills that
  are difficult to teach by conventional
  methods;
● cause the children to be actively engaged
  in their learning;
● be flexible enough to cope with varying
  levels of ability;
● have sufficient support material.

It shouldn't . . .
● be merely drill and practice;
● be a teacher replacement;
● be too difficult to operate!

5 A program should:

1
2
3
4
5

After discussion, decide on your agreed priorities.

Finally . . .

Computers are not superhuman. They break down. They make
errors – sometimes dangerous ones. There is nothing magical about
them, and they are assuredly not 'spirits' or 'souls' in our environment.
Yet with all these qualifications, they remain among the most amazing and
unsettling of human achievements, for they enhance our muscle power,
and we do not know where our own minds will ultimately lead us.[5]

7 English with Drama?

Case study: 'we don't go near enough what matters to kids'

It is a Tuesday afternoon in March 1984, Gavin Bolton[1] is working with a group of thirty fourth-years from a Reading comprehensive school. They are all studying CSE Drama – and are indeed expecting something 'dramatic'! The space in which they are to work is a large one but Gavin has confined them at the outset to a circle of chairs. In a very quiet voice, he introduces himself and they are gently prodded into reciprocating: a flurry of names sweeping around the circle.

'Do you know what you're here for?'

There is a fidgeting silence. Then he explains what his intentions and hopes are, concluding with a crucial question – 'What sort of Drama are you used to?'

'All sorts . . .'

'I want to learn from *you* what you want the drama to be about . . .

Gavin is now firmly in the circle, waiting for the silence to yield an idea that everyone can seize upon.

'Torture!'

'What kind?'

'Different kinds – emotional and physical.'

Gavin seems taken aback momentarily, but covers it by talking, drawing parallels between physical torture and mental torment; he holds their attention, at one stage sharing with them an anecdote from his own life. Then, as if he has made a decision, he asks for further suggestions, emphasising that what they choose to do must involve them all.

'How do you feel about handling mental torture? Any reasons why we shouldn't do it?'

Silence.

'Can you suggest a way of checking?'

'A vote.'

The vote is unanimously approving. The decision appears to have been reached, but Gavin claims not to be happy even now and asks if they can talk it through further.

'I want you,' he says, 'to get a lot from it. Can you give me time to think?'

So saying, he falls silent; their patience is sought and they obligingly sit and wait.

Eventually, he chooses to seize the nettle. 'I'm going to work with you in a way that I've never worked before.'

They are to be patients in a mental hospital. Gavin moves a chair into the centre of the circle; normally, when working with patients, he is intending to focus the problem upon himself, but this time working with school children, he has no such intention. The chair remains empty until the time 'when we are ready'. The immediate objective is to focus down on one root cause of the problem of mental illness. He throws out two possibilities – drug addiction, gambling – and then invites them to talk it over amongst themselves. Gavin moves around, picking up the threads of a dozen conversations and then writing the suggestions on the board:

Gambling	Wife bashing	Suicide	Drunkenness	Drugs	Phobias	Child Abuse

They vote:

7	deleted	12	2	2	2	1

On a revote, the almost unanimous opinion of the group is that they should concentrate upon suicide. All this negotiation and genuine democracy has taken a long time and there is a feeling that Gavin has been rail-roaded into a situation which he would not have chosen for himself. That, of course, is partly the point! He admits now to be beginning the process of identifying the protagonist . . . and then:

'*You* are the people who were his fellow pupils . . .'

He asks them to work in pairs, still operating within the confines (or security) of the circle. From this point, it is clear that Gavin has changed the direction of the drama: the 'patients' aspect is lost and the focus is turned on their own experience . . .

'Don't be too serious about it – use a light touch. One of you is a gossip and enjoys having a good natter about . . . what's his name? Let's have a name that *isn't* one of you. "Bob?" OK, Bob then. One of you is the gossip; the other disapproves. You are talking about what has happened to Bob.'

The pairs seize the opportunity to explore this new territory. After a while, Gavin calls them back to him.

'OK. Why is Bob driven to it?'

There are various suggestions, the most provocative of which is 'Spots!' It is an offering intended to sabotage; the accompanying giggle highlights the moment as a dangerous one. Gavin decides to slow the process down and respond to the challenge.

'Think about the "underneath" of that and your view of yourself.

Suicides see themselves as spotted in some way.'

It is a curiously memorable moment: a moment when all the minds in the room shift with the tension in the air.

At what feels the 'right' moment, Gavin takes them back to the developing story:

'Let's go back to that moment in Bob's life when it all began – we need a Bob to sit in that central chair.'

Sure enough, someone volunteers, though as yet he prefers to sit with the rest in the circle. Gavin asks for a 'mother' now and presses them to reach such decisions quickly; he sets up a situation where Bob realises for the first time that his parents' relationship is under real stress. The volunteer mother and son improvise across the circle until Gavin stops them, commenting on the quality of the subtext. Armed with a volunteer 'father', Bob plays a scene in which son quizzes father about his behaviour and recent whereabouts . . . As the scene ends, Gavin asks the father where, in fact, he had been.

'At my secretary's house!' he says with a smirk.

Gavin turns to Bob:

'Can you cope with being in the middle yet?' Bob, with a shy, self-conscious shrug, moves to the central chair and plays a scene with his best friend in which Bob is left in little doubt as to what is the cause of his parents' difficulties.

'What would Bob do next?'

'Ask his Mum or his Dad?'

'Which?'

The verdict of the group is emphatically that Bob would want to talk the matter through with his mother. Gavin asks the group to pair off and, for the first time, to move outside the safety of the chairs.

'One of you is Bob and one is the mother. How does Bob bring the matter up with her? Have a chat with your partner and decide where all this is happening. Oh yes, and it'll be left to each individual mother to decide exactly how much of the truth you reveal.'

The class works well on these 'scenes' (interestingly, that is what Gavin calls them, despite the theatrical connotations of the word). Although the class has been absorbed in what has been going on, they are obviously pleased to be on their feet and doing. Significantly, there is no anxiety about males playing females (or indeed female Bobs!); the reason is simply Gavin's certainty of touch and absolute seriousness – mutual respect. Eventually he draws them back in, asking the original Bob and mother to play the scene. It is a sharp fragment only, the mother snapping at Bob until he retreats all too easily. Gavin makes a joke of it – and then asks a critical question:

'Did you mean to cut him off like that?'

'No,' she says, 'I would've admitted to being in a bad patch or something.'

There is a short general discussion in which the class is asked to compare their own versions with what they have just seen. Gavin is now anxious about time and admits to the children that he is feeling pressed.

'But what other pressures would Bob face?'

'School!'

With time closing in, Gavin seems to be indicating possibilities for further development; certainly his questioning and suggestions are 'tighter' than earlier in the session:

'This could happen to anyone,' he says, this after a scene in which Bob is unwittingly pushed nearer the edge by three of his schoolfriends talking about their own examination success and Bob's apparently abject failure. 'There's only time now to *discuss* the alternatives. It's interesting to think about who's to blame for a start.' Bob is asked back into the circle and Gavin compliments all of the students on their work and thanks them too. An hour and a half has passed.

On two counts it was an artificial 'lesson'. Gavin Bolton and that class were to meet but once; there was the complicating factor that they were new to each other, which can be advantageous in some ways, but certainly makes continuity and security difficult to achieve. Secondly, there was a second circle of chairs around the perimeter of the space with some forty teachers watching, scribbling notes and, at one unfortunately inopportune moment, laughing. The effect of that hyper-critical audience must have been inhibiting, though neither Gavin nor the children appeared ruffled by the experience – indeed, the students carefully avoided eye-contact with the outsiders. The forty teachers included some who would regard themselves above all else as teachers of Drama – Drama trained and therefore 'specialists'; others who teach English and Drama, and yet more who fall into neither category: primary teachers of course, and one or two from other disciplines and a secondary Deputy Head brought along for the good of his soul! The mixed nature of the group highlights a problem that haunts most English departments:

- *Who* does the Drama teaching?

And the problem doesn't rest there:

- *Who* does the school play?
- *Where* is the Drama taught?
- What *is* Drama anyway?

Before leaving Gavin Bolton, it is worth quoting two of the comments he made in the concluding session. Both his comments came while answering queries about the content of the drama he had just been initiating:

- 'The most creative work can emerge from the narrowest of parameters' and

- 'We don't go near enough what matters to kids.'

Developing Drama

There are those who would argue fiercely that Drama is an essential, not an optional, part of English. Yet watching Gavin Bolton work, without any reference to anything other than 'the Drama', it is clear that Drama is both a separate and a highly significant element in the whole curriculum, as well as being a method through which *real* learning – through participation (you *know* because you've been there) – takes place. Equally contentious is the distinction to be drawn between Drama and Theatre: presentation, from the showing of polished improvisation to the formality of the school play, has its place, but for many people, including many Headteachers, the *process* of Drama has come very much a poor second to the 'high-profile' product.

In reality things don't become resolved so easily: too many constraints can militate against the strong Drama department that recognises its special relationship with English, underpins the school's policy for active learning across the curriculum, and yet can come up with a sell-out production of *West Side Story* or *Gregory's Girl*. The only real solution lies in exploiting the situation as it stands and not clinging on to philosophical convictions that bear little relation to the school in its present state of development. One thing *is* certain, however: those children who leave school at sixteen or eighteen without the experience of any kind of Drama are at a disadvantage – and, in the absence of anyone else, it is likely to be the English Department that attempts to right the wrong.

A variety of approaches
SCHOOL 1

> For a number of years, since I was appointed Head of English, most of our school's Drama has been taught by our Senior Mistress. She's very good actually, but it's not Drama as I know it – lots of movement work, a massive school production every year, no Drama at all after the first year. I want to introduce a CSE course, but there are a number of problems – who teaches it? How do we get kids to opt for it in the fourth year if they've not had Drama since the first year? How do we broaden the kind of Drama the kids do?

SCHOOL 2

> I have no contact with the English department in our place at all – well, who would want to! My (Drama) department consists of three of us and we have the use of the purpose-built studio and school hall. Drama is taught to all pupils in the first three years – in hour-long lessons – and

we have large numbers of pupils opting for CSE in the fourth year. We don't run an O level course, because we're very enthusiastic about CSE and we've done a lot of work educating parents about what we do. There are regular demonstrations of classroom-based, practical Drama work in the evenings for parents to see. The next obvious development, I suppose, is in the sixth form.

SCHOOL 3

I was appointed with such high hopes, though I should have remembered how the Head looked when I asked about the possibility of a scale 2 right at the end of the interview. He looked sick! What he wanted was someone to build up Drama, do two productions a year, and teach two other subjects – all for a scale 1. There's no Drama studio, only a hut – which I'm not sure if I'm getting next year – and the Hall which I can't use if there's exams on, or if the PE staff are in there because it's raining.

SCHOOL 4

I keep telling the Head that unless we appoint on a scale 2, we won't get anybody. They all stay a year and get pregnant – well, wouldn't you teaching Drama to classes of thirty in a hut which is frostbound in winter and like a greenhouse in summer? This year we've all taught some, but reluctantly really and only to keep the subject alive. We need help and yet the Head makes promises that we've come to recognise as empty.

SCHOOL 5

Notes on Drama for intending applicants to a scale 1 Drama post:

In formal terms, all children in years 1 to 3 now receive some Drama teaching and an option course for years 4 and 5 is being established. In more informal terms, Drama is part of the regular vocabulary in departmental discussion and a constant point of reference in planning as well as a palpable influence throughout the school in its own right.

In wide educational terms there are a number of aspects with which we engage: the cultivation of harmonious working in small and large groups, self-awareness, expression of individual and collective ideas, responsibility, patience and tolerance, problem-solving and decision-making. There are, of course, specific applications within the department like the exploration of character and interpretation of texts, and one major task now is to integrate Drama into 'straight' English more fully than at present . . . Facilities are not outstanding.

Problems like these are commonplace and usually they can be traced back to difficulties of space and personnel – personalities that don't mesh, or views of Drama (and the world probably) that do not accord with each other.

Drama development within the school

Strategies	Notes
1 Involve the staff in *practical* in-service activity.	Not just 'English' staff.
2 Link Drama work with other subject areas.	Don't just stick to History!
3 Diversify the kind of school productions on offer.	To include as many kids and staff as possible.
4 Get Drama on to the fourth- and fifth-year timetable as an option.	May need 'phasing in' – the students will need to know what 'Drama' means before opting for it: this means some Drama in year 3.
5 Ensure that Drama is on the agenda of departmental and Heads of Department meetings.	(i) *Specific* issues to be discussed. (ii) Someone needs to take responsibility for supporting Drama at senior/middle management meetings.
6 Put on demonstrations of practical drama work for parents to see.	Include a range of work from as many year groups as possible.
7 Invite in theatre-in-education and children's theatre teams on a regular basis.	Ensure the quality of the company first by checking with colleagues from other schools, or the local adviser.
8 Take work out to local primary schools, old people's homes, etc.	Or, more ambitious, arrange a week on tour elsewhere in the country.
9 Make sure that *only* those teachers who want to be involved are time-tabled to teach Drama.	Having arranged that, make certain that the team meets, shares and collaborates.
10 On those occasions when a Drama teacher is away, ensure that the work set is (a) demanding of the kids but (b) manageable for the substitute.	(i) No play readings around the class. (ii) Remember it's part of educating the rest of the staff about Drama.

Strategies	*Notes*
11 Press for one-hour or 70–minute lessons, rather than single periods of 35 or 40 minutes.	(i) Single lessons exacerbate the problem of maintaining continuity in Drama. (ii) A double lesson once a fortnight may be preferable.
12 Be involved in any LEA-wide Drama organisation that exists.	If one doesn't exist, start one: Drama teachers need mutual support.

Developing the Drama curriculum
Starting points can be:

Class discussion
  A script
    A short story or poem
      Documents
        Letters
          Music
            Photographs
            Pictures
              A map
                Emotions
                  Attitudes
                    Situation/role cards[2]
                  Time and space
                    Costume, props, lights, set, space
                  An issue
                    A problem
                    Tableaux[3]
                      Teacher-in-role[4]
                    Games

It would be a useful starting point in itself for a department to discuss successful occasions when they have used one or more of the above in stimulating Drama. In practice, a lot of Drama lessons begin with a series of games, ostensibly as a warm up, but arguably to defer the moment when the *real* work begins!

At the heart of the lesson, or the sequence of lessons, must be the nature of the relationship that exists between the teacher and all permutations of the group – and beyond the relationship is the contract forged between the two. What the teacher brings and the contribution of the children, both collectively and individually, are of equal weight in the enterprise:

The teacher brings . . .	*The children bring . . .*
Choice of content and form.	An awareness of what matters to them.
Alternatives.	A knowledge of each other.
An ability to negotiate.	Skills of movement and language.
An ability to shape.	Unpretentious judgement.
Imagination.	Imagination.
Timing.	Enthusiasm.
Ideas.	Ideas.
Awareness of time and space.	Cultures.
Control.	Trust.
Sensitivity.	Experiences.

Where is it leading?

Discussion.
Reflection.
Polishing.
Showing the work, sharing.
Photos.
Reporting.
Tape.
Writing.
Video and film.
Art.
Music.

Ideally, the process is completed by further stimulus. Go back to the starting points again (page 104). The aim is for *continuity*.

The child's experience of Drama in your school

- Is there a syllabus which genuinely reflects practice and to which *all* the staff teaching Drama have contributed?

- Are the children involved in the process of discussing Drama? Are they asked to offer opinions about the Drama they are experiencing?

- Is the work varied? Does it draw upon the school curriculum?

- Are the numbers opting for Drama in the fourth year healthy? Or is there an 'exploitable' movement from the parents/children asking for an option in the fourth year (or the sixth)?

- Is there a place for mime, dance, and movement work?

What do you do if . . .
The questionnaire in figure 19 has proved an interesting focus for discussing the *practicalities* of teaching Drama. I have included one (primary) teacher's response.

Figure 19   What do you do if . . . ?

	1	If Drama has a low status in your school?	Invite TIE groups into the school; show how Drama can relate across the subject barriers; prove that it's important, show how the children benefit.
	2	When you have to work in an inappropriate space?	Lots of Drama can be done sitting down! Start with that type of session. The important thing is to make a start.
	3	When you suffer constant interruptions?	It depends on the type of interruptions – children learn to ignore canteen noises, etc. in the hall. I like to incorporate teachers who interrupt into the Drama!
	4	When the children are very inhibited?	Take it gently; now is the time to use games. Start by using only things within their experience. Give praise. Don't force 'showing' the work.
WHAT	5	With a very boisterous class?	Use it – by incorporating it into the Drama.
	6	With children whose concentration is poor?	Do lots of things that are fairly short; try to increase concentration by improving motivation.
DO	7	To mix children who always want to work a) with their friends b) with members of the same sex?	Use 'Mill and Grab' to fix the groups: everyone mills around – teacher calls number, e.g. five – everyone gets into groups of five – those left out at the end form their own group. The *speed* of the game stops the kids plotting to be with friends, etc.
	8	When the children regurgitate popular TV programmes instead of thinking for themselves?	Choose subjects offered by the kids with care; accept more readily suggestions from children who are *not* offering tired TV ideas.
YOU	9	About fighting?	A few sessions on stage fights always go well: slow the action down?
	10	With children who trivialise the work?	Praise and elevate the work of those children who are not trivialising the work.
DO	11	With the child who no one wants to work with?	Use the Drama to soothe the situation; use the cooperative children to help; use groupings that make it impossible; try to pinpoint the reason and resolve it!
	12	With the bolshy child or the chosen isolate who does not want to take part?	It depends! It may be possible to let them take charge and lead – it's really a matter of motivation – knowing the children helps! Sometimes you can pretend you haven't noticed and the child will join in unobtrusively.
	13	With the child who dominates?	Put dominating children together in the same group – sometimes . . Work in mode of 'beginning, middle and end' so that different children decide how it begins, progresses and finishes.
	14	When you realise a lesson has fallen apart?	ADMIT IT! See if you can recognise why; can you use that information to get it going again? Can the children help?
	15	About working with sensitive material?	Use your own moral code as a guide. Be careful: protect the children that can be hurt.
	16	When you only have 35 minutes?	Choose material that can be contained in the period of time – try to stop at a convenient section and allow time for discussion, either to consolidate or find a way forward next time.
	17	When you feel like death?!	Let the children take the lead early in the lesson.

Finally . . .

Though drama is probably discussed more today in terms of teaching and learning than it has been in the past, it is far from being fully exploited in our schools. It continues to limp along, never quite able to show its potential because the system, as it stands, preserves jealously the 'one class, one teacher' syndrome, the 'everybody has to be the same age in the group' syndrome, the 'teacher has the secrets' syndrome, the 'we can't have more than one person making decisions' syndrome, the 'let's keep everything in short periods' syndrome, and, above all, the 'let's not have too many children surprising the teacher' syndrome.

'Drama and learning' by Dorothy Heathcote[5]

8 Making Decisions in a Changing World

As Dorothy Heathcote's remarks, quoted at the conclusion of the previous chapter, indicate, schools are not designed to cope with rapid change, still less to promote it. While the complexities of life increase, schools appear to change only at the behest of the Manpower Services Commission. Children can see through the system more readily – and earlier: one eight-year-old told me recently: 'Going to school is silly really. The teachers already know the answers but we have to do it for them.'

English departments are less guilty than most of failing to open up the world for pupils. On those occasions when our consciences twinge, it is easy to blame the examination system and forget to ask questions about our own practice that tests its worth. In English teaching, like many other invaluable activities, certainty can all too readily turn to narrow overconfidence; ease to a languid tedium. It is necessary to question oneself and each other – and the children – constantly: to look at the world, its methods of communication, its political structures, its art, its cultures, and adapt our patterns of teaching English to accommodate those external changes, preserve what is unalterable and seize upon the needs, experience and energy of the children who pass through our classrooms. It is not just a question of helping pupils 'learning to learn, learning to live, coping with people/machine interfaces and coping with change',[1] important as these things undoubtedly are; it is also about fostering and shaping their own experience, making sense of the world, past, present and future, learning to trust their immeasurable latent talent for self-expression. These are concerns central to the child's experience in school and prime concerns for teachers of English. Above all – and this must be unchanging and inalienable – it is teachers of English alone in school who provide varied and sustained opportunities for pupils to explore language, to share it, to be moved by it, and to learn about life through its use. The nature of that language will change, so will its users, but English teachers will always be concerned to make readers through dialogue or discourse; to develop the craft of writing; to foster an understanding of, and a sensitivity to, what is said; to know what language can do.

It is easy to be complacent and to assume you know and they don't. I once read, with some trepidation, to my fifth-year CSE group, the following poem. 'You probably won't like it,' I said, apologetically, knowing the bell would save me.

He always
He always wanted to explain things, but no one cared,
So he drew.
Sometimes he would just draw and it wasn't anything.
He wanted to carve it in stone or write it in the sky.
He would lie out on the grass and look upon the sky,
it would be only the sky and the things inside him
that needed saying
And it was after that he drew the picture,
It was a beautiful picture. He kept it under his pillow and
Would let no one see it.
And he would look at it every night and think about it
And when it was dark and his eyes were closed he could see it still.
And it was all of him and he loved it.

When he started school he brought it with him,
Not to show anyone, but just to have with him like
a friend.
It was funny about school
He sat in a square brown desk like all the other square desks
and he thought it would be red.
And his room was a square brown room, like all those other rooms.
And it was tight and close. And stiff.
He hated to hold the pencil of chalk, with his arms stiff
and his feet flat on the floor, stiff with the teacher
Watching and watching.
The teacher came and spoke to him.
She told him to wear a tie like all the other boys.
He said he didn't like them and she said it didn't matter.
After that he drew. And he drew all yellow and
it was the way he felt about morning,
And it was beautiful.
The teacher came and smiled at him. 'What's this?' she said.
'Why don't you draw something like Ken's drawing? Isn't it beautiful?'
After that his mother bought him a tie and he always drew airplanes
and rocket ships
like everyone else.
And he threw the old pictures away.
And when he lay out alone looking at the sky, it was big and blue,
and all of everything that he wasn't anymore.
He was square and brown inside and his hands were stiff.

And he was like everyone else. All the things inside him that needed
saying didn't need it anymore.
It had stopped pushing. It was crushed.
Stiff
Like everything else.

I should have known better. There was a silence that lasted for half a
minute or so, then one of the boys said:
'It's just like that.'
And they all agreed.

The decisions are yours!

What follows, as a conclusion to the main body of the book, is a
simulation 'game' based on an imaginary (but, hopefully, realistic)
English department. It is best done as a departmental activity, with key
information released by the leader of the session at certain points
(marked *).

* Part 1:

The John Holt School. Headmaster: Jack Ginsberg BSc. (Econ.).

The John Holt School is an 11–18 comprehensive serving the
southwest corner of the county. Selection was abolished in 1974 and the
school now has a fully comprehensive intake with a total of 950 students
on roll – of these 89 are in the sixth form. Numbers are not expected to
fall significantly in the near future.

The area served by the school is mainly rural with a certain amount of
varied industry. There is a large council development in the town. The
school itself was built in two phases: as a small secondary modern with
buildings completed in 1962; and a new block incorporating an
administrative suite of offices as well as a staffroom, library, music and
dance studio. There is a suite of three English classrooms in the old
buildings, as well as a small office for the Head of Department's use, a
bookstore and resources cupboard.

The pastoral organisation of the school is on a house basis with Heads
of House whose work is to coordinate a team of tutors in dealing with
the welfare, progress and discipline of the pupils. Heads of Department
are expected to be responsible for standards of discipline within their
own subject specialism.

THE ENGLISH DEPARTMENT

There are six full-time teachers in the department, including three
graduates. In addition, there are three members of staff who teach some
junior English. The department includes within it a small Drama
department under a Head of Drama (scale 2).

English is taught in mixed ability groups throughout the first three years; thereafter O level and CSE are taught separately, while English Literature is, at present, an option. A level English is well established (some twenty students) and there are also City and Guilds and O level courses operating in the lower (one-year) sixth. The retiring Head of Department has recently chaired a working party on 'Language across the curriculum'.

Before taking up your appointment as Head of English (in January), you receive *two* letters, one from Charles King, Deputy Head (Curriculum), and the other from the Headmaster, Jack Ginsberg. Ginsberg is – despite his degree in Economics! – an ex-Head of English; he is forceful, interfering and enjoys pushing paper across his desk!

* THE STAFF

From Charles King (Deputy Head, Curriculum):
I thought the following information (confidential of course!) might be helpful.

Second in English (scale 2):   *George Heyer*

         – Aged 39.

         – Graduated lower 2nd from Hull.

         – Put in for your job; wasn't interviewed.

         – Very active in the NAS/UWT; school rep.

         – Runs the school bookshop (it's virtually dead).

Head of Drama (scale 2):   *Harry Painter*

         – Aged 26.

         – Central School (failed actor!)

         – Empire builder.

         – Sees English and Drama as separate areas.

The rest: *Maurice Duffy*

         – Scale 4.

         – Head of House.

– Aged 40.

– College trained.

– Strong on discipline; very over-worked (aren't we all!).

– Anti-mixed ability.

– Aggressive!

Margaret Cassidy

– Scale 1.

– Aged 23.

– Just married.

– Just out of her probationary year.

– Also teaches Drama.

– Can't spell.

Rosamund Moth

– Scale 1.

– 1st class graduate (London).

– Aged 22.

– Appointed for potential with 6th form.

– Poor discipline, especially 4th and 5th year.

– Keen to develop the school magazine.

– A poor organiser.

– Probationer.

In addition, the following teachers 'do' some English:

Yours truly!

The Head (when he's here)

Iris Murdoch (Girls' PE)

A final thought: the Head is keen on you having a departmental meeting to consider the Language Policy situation as soon as possible. Could you concoct an agenda for that meeting?

See you in January,

Charles King.

FROM THE HEAD

I enclose for your perusal the first- and second-year Stocklist – as I believe you requested.

The Governors have asked for a meeting soon after you have arrived on the work of the department. Obviously they will give you a month or so to find your feet. I believe the root of the problem is concern over Assessment and Marking: a Parent-governor is very anxious about 'the non-marking of English work'!

Could you devise a brief statement about this and suggest a possible approach to the problem?

I notice incidentally that the last English syllabus is dated 1967; perhaps your statement could serve as an introduction to a revised – no, a new! – syllabus? Throw a few ideas down on paper for me.

Finally, your capitation for the present financial year is £1,500, of which just over £850 remains. It would be wise to come to us prepared with priorities for spending.

Looking forward to seeing you in January,

Jack Ginsberg,

Headmaster

Enc. Stocklist.

English department stocklist: years 1 and 2

Language and Coursebooks

Art of English I	Mansfield	60 copies
Art of English II	"	"
Art of English III	"	"
Explore and Express I		30 copies
Explore and Express II		"
English First I		27
English First II		30
English Through Experience I		17
English Through Experience II		45

Fiction

The Silver Sword	30 copies
Animal Farm	"
Grandad With Snails – Baldwin	"
The Otterbury Incident – Lewis	"
Kes	"
The Guardians	"
The Pigman – Zindel	"
Tom's Midnight Garden	"
Storymakers I and II	"
The Goalkeeper's Revenge	"

Poetry

Touchstones I and II
Dragonsteeth
Themes: Men and Beasts
        Conflict

Drama texts

Scene scripts
Julius Caesar
The Long, the Short and the Tall
The Chicken Run

* Part 2: In-tray

It is now the end of November and you have been in post for over two terms; your staff in the department remain unchanged. It being Monday morning, you have a well-earned double free period during which you can tackle the following items in your in-tray. Find an order of priority and act where possible!

1 To: English Department
   From: JG
   Date: 25th November 198–

Please note the contents of the attached letter. I would be grateful for some notes or, better still, a draft of my reply!

22nd November 198–

Dear Mr Ginsberg,

I am writing to protest most forcibly about the books that children such as mine are forced to study at school. I am horrified that such a book as 'Kes' should be used in your school when we have a culture of good literature like we do in England. I know language like this exists, but why do you use literature that soils instead of really educating a child's mind? Language like this is too easily accepted in your classrooms, especially by your English teachers.

I look forward to an early reply. A copy of this letter has been sent to the Chairman of Education Committee and the Chairman of Governors.

Yours faithfully,
C. Oddfellow.

2 To: Headmaster
   From: George Heyer
   Copy to: Head of English
   Date: 28th November

For some time, the department has felt thwarted in its attempts to develop a genuine passion for writing in the children by the sad practice of many staff using 'impositions' and 'essays' as punishments. How can children be expected to understand the subtle(!) difference between the craft of writing, nurtured by a caring teacher, building on and developing their experience, their view of the world, and, conversely, fatuous 'essays' written to satisfy some teacher's sadistic whim? Sorry, overstated I know, but we do feel strongly about this! Do you have any objections to me sending out a memorandum to all staff asking for comments?
   G.H.

3 To: Head of English
   From: Charles King
   Date: 24th November

Any help you can give me on this?

To: Deputy Head (Curriculum)

Dear Sir,
Ever since our son James came to your school, we have been concerned that staff appear unable to understand his problems. I shouldn't need to remind you that he has always found English confusing. Imagine our feelings then when, in looking through his exercise book, we find remarks like 'Why is this homework so like Peter's?' James does *not* cheat. Moreover, Miss Cassidy appears to have *no* understanding of constructive marking: no spellings are corrected, there is no 'mark' and her comments I find offensive, while James, who is a sensitive boy, is clearly very upset by them.
   As a parent governor, I intend to raise this matter *again* at next week's Governors' meeting. Why *is* there no apparent marking policy in the school? In view of the forthcoming Inspectors' visit, perhaps it is high time the issue was resolved.
   Yours faithfully,
   Anna Riddle.

4 To: Head of English
   From: Head
   Date: 29th November

Come into my office for a moment today, can you? I've received rather an offensive note from George Heyer.
   J.G.

5 To: Head of English
   From: Head of Modern Languages
   Copy to: Deputy Head (Curric.)

At our last departmental meeting we unanimously agreed that the time
has come for us to press more firmly for a return to formal grammar. I
know we've talked about this before, usually over a drink in the 'Duck'
after a parents' evening (!), but we are now at the point when a stand must
be taken. We find it very unusual these days if a child knows what a 'verb'
is; 'tense' they associate with camping, and a real knowledge of the
language of grammar is unknown. We *must* discuss this properly. I have
taken the liberty of inviting Ray Warren, the County's Modern Languages
Adviser, to spend the day with us tomorrow. Perhaps we can have a
chat – all of us – over lunch tomorrow in order to set things rolling?

6 To: Head of English
   From: Charles King
   Date: 29th November

An interesting memo to me from the Head (attached). Any reactions on
either the computer or Library fronts?

7 Internal memorandum:
   To: Deputy Head
   From: Head

I have just received a request from Harry Jarman (Adviser for Computer
Education) asking me to indicate what steps we're taking to establish a
policy for Computer Assisted Learning. In particular, he wants to know
how the Computer suite will service the needs of *all* departments ...
Over to you! Can you give me some indication of our line on this?

    On a related theme, I'm increasingly concerned about the failure of our
library to cater for the needs of the whole school: too often if feels like an
expensive adjunct to the English Department. Shouldn't it be more
clearly at the heart of our work? Why is the Science section so thin? Why
do the English Department seem to be the only department who take the
pupils in there on a regular basis? What are you going to *do* about it?
Answer in note form by 4 p.m.!

* Part 3: Developing policy?
Eighteen months on!

(i)   Maurice Duffy has finally got his Deputy Headship – not
     before time! Draft a job specification for his successor.

(ii) From the Head:

Would you (with help from two or three others) plan a twenty minute presentation for our new parents' evening which *demonstrates* what the department does/can do to improve reading skills as well as the reading habit? I'd like some thought given to 'reluctant' readers . . .

(iii) And finally:

Internal memorandum
To: Head of English
From: Head
Date: 20th December

Firstly: Can you suggest a decent novel for me to read over the holidays? I seem to have got out of the habit of reading! Something that will be good for me.

Secondly: Who said:[2] 'Your mother tells me that you do not know how to read, and are refusing to learn. It surprises me very much that a little girl of six should not know how to read, and expects to be read to. It is disgraceful, and you must promise me to learn at once; if you don't, I shall have to put your father and mother in prison.'

The young lady in question says of him:

'I was startled and frightened by his threat and at the same time very puzzled that a poet could put people in prison. I asked father whether he could put him in prison. Father hesitated: "No, I don't think he could, although he *is* a Government Inspector of Schools."'!

Notes
and References

1 The purpose of English teaching

1 *Best Laid Plans: English Teachers at Work*, ed. S. Horner, Longman for the Schools Council (1983).
2 *Continuity in Secondary English* by David Jackson, Methuen (1982).
3 *Writing and the Writer* by Frank Smith, Heinemann (1982).
4 I am indebted to John Taylor HMI for drawing my attention to Kafka's remark.
5 Cf. The 'areas of experience' itemised in *Curriculum 11–16* (1978).
6 *Thunder and Lightnings* by Jan Mark, Puffin (1976).
7 *Reading, How to* by Herbert Kohl, Penguin (1974).
8 *The Disappearing Dais* by Frank Whitehead, Chatto (1966).
9 *English Teaching since 1965 – How much Growth?* by David Allen, Heinemann (1980).
10 B. Hollingworth in *Use of English*, spring 1974, vol. 25/3.
11 I am indebted to Patrick Sanders, Deputy Head at Wallingford School, Oxfordshire, for providing me with this case study. I should add that it is *not* based on the work of any teachers at Wallingford, or with whom he has worked. Any resemblance is, as they say, entirely coincidental!
12 The format for fig. 3 was suggested by *Best Laid Plans*, op. cit.
13 *Sharing Resources* by Averil Brooker, booklet No. 2 in the 'Learning about Learning' series published by Wiltshire Education Department and organised by Pat D'Arcy, Wiltshire's English Adviser.
14 *Talking about Equality: the use and importance of discussion in multi-cultural education* by Robin Richardson, Adviser for Multi-cultural Education, Berkshire. Cambridge Journal of Education Vol. 12 No. 2 Easter (1982).
15 'Class of 62' by Polly Toynbee, *Guardian*, 23 January 1984.
16 *Saville* by David Storey, Jonathan Cape (1976), Penguin (1978).

2 Priorities

1 Gene Kemp, quoted in *The Times Educational Supplement*, 30 September 1983.
2 I am indebted to Gene Kemp and Damion Speight for this letter.

3   *Readers and Texts 1: The Reading Process*, compiled and edited by Bob Moy for the English Centre, ILEA (1980).
4   Comments by a teacher on a fourth-year CSE group – set 4 out of 6!
5   For more on this see *Books and Reading Development* by Jennie Ingham, Heinemann (1981), which details the Bradford Book Flood Experiment.
6   This list of questions is adapted from a curriculum guidelines document drawn up in Berkshire as a result of DES circular 6/81.
7   'Comprehension – Bringing it Back Alive' by Bob Moy and Mike Raleigh, *The English Magazine*, autumn 1980.
8   One nine-year-old girl, on reading this, claimed: 'That's nothing. I bet I've read my Laura Ingalls Wilder that many times!'
9   *Children, Language and Literature*, Open University (1982).
10 *NATE News*, National Association for the Teaching of English, spring 1983.
11 See pages 73–74.
12 Southern Regional Examinations Board CSE English Literature (Syllabus R), 1983.
13 A quotation borrowed from an anonymous teacher somewhere in southern England!
14 *The Whitsun Weddings* by Philip Larkin, Faber (1964).
15 *Here Today*, Hutchinson Educational (1963).
16 Both articles appear in *Children, Language and Literature*, op. cit.
17 *The Effective Use of Reading*, ed. Lunzer and Gardner, Heinemann (1979). *Learning from the Written Word* ed. Lunzer and Gardner, Oliver and Boyd (1984).
18 Ho Thien's last ten lines are:

> And the boy knew everything,
> He knew everything about them, the caves,
> the trails the hidden places and the names,
> and in the moment that he cried out
> in that same instant,
> protected by frail tears
> far stronger than any wall of steel,
> they passed everywhere
> like tigers
> across the High Plateau.

19 Published by *London Magazine Editions* (1975).
20 *The Tidy House* by Carolyn Steadman, Virago (1982), p. 99.
21 *Aspects of Secondary Education*, DES (1979).
22 *Writing: Teachers and Children at Work* by Donald Graves, Heinemann (1983).
23 Bernard Harrison in *Learning through Writing*, NFER/Nelson (1983), quotes Doris Lessing: 'you change as you write, you change yourself, you change the way you think'.
24 *From Communication to Curriculum* by Douglas Barnes, Penguin (1976).
25 *Aspects of Secondary Education*, op. cit, Ch. 6; quoted in *Bullock Revisited* HMI document, published by DES (1982).
26 Faber (1984), p. 45.

27 *Sunday Times*, April 1983.
28 *Continuity in Secondary English*, op. cit.
29 *Guardian*, 6 June 1984.
30 The list was drawn up for an in-service course by Elizabeth Gunner, author of *A Handbook for Teaching African Literature*, Heinemann (1984).
31 After Preiswerk R. (1980) *The Slant of the Pen: Racism in Children's Books*, World Council of Churches (1980); quoted in *Children, Language and Literature*, op. cit., p. 27.
32 *The School Leaver* by Michael McMillan, Black Ink Publications (1978), p. 16.
33 From *Bluefoot Traveller*, ed. James Berry, Harrap (1981).
34 Devised by Bob Moy.
35 Published by Topliner (1976).
36 Published by Faber (1958).
37 'The Appropriate Slant' in *The Times Educational Supplement*, 8 July 1983.
38 This section owes a lot to Elizabeth Gunner, Veronica Treacher and others who have been active in recent ATCAL (Association for the Teaching of Caribbean, African and Associated Literature) conferences in Berkshire; and to Sandra Hann, the Coordinator of the 'Fiction and Multicultural Education' project based in Slough (1983–4).
39 *The Tidy House*, op. cit., p. 139.
40 *The Machine Gunners* by Robert Westall, Macmillan (1975), Puffin (1977).
41 *Doing Things in and about the Home*, produced by teachers based on Maidenhead Teachers' Centre, Serawood Press (1983).
42 *The Practical Princess and other Liberating Tales* by Jay Williams, Hippo (1983).
43 *Kidder's Luck*, by J. Common, Turnstile Press (1951); quoted in *The Challenge for the Comprehensive School: Culture, Curriculum and Community* by David H. Hargreaves, Routledge & Kegan Paul (1982).

3 Language: diversity, awareness and policies

1 The phrase – and the technique – was suggested by Professor David Crystal of Reading University.
2 Spring 1984.
3 *Bullock Revisited*, op. cit.
4 'Making It Happen', *The Times Educational Supplement*.
5 *The Foundations of Language* by Andrew Wilkinson, Oxford University Press (1971).
6 Ibid.
7 I am grateful to Robin Richardson for permission to use this material.
8 I owe a debt to Peter Allsop, Head of English at Fernhill School, Farnborough, Hampshire, for telling me about the teaching methods explored in this unit.
9 W. H. Mittins in a paper called 'What is Correctness?' in *Language Perspectives*, ed. B. Wade, Heinemann (1982).

4 Coping with pressure: organisation and strategies

1 *The Bullock Report* (1974), p. 230.
2 Macmillan (1972), Picador (1982).
3 Op. cit., p. 33.
4 Michael Joseph (1980), Corgi (1981).
5 The Kennet School, Thatcham, Berkshire.
6 *Language Across the Transition* by M. Creasey, F. Findlay and B. Walsh, Longman for the Schools Council (1983).

5 Evaluation

1 Both of these quotations were brought to my attention by teachers involved in a recent (1984) course on 'Evaluating English Work' organised by the Southern Conference for Development Work in English.
2 There is an example of an English department concerning itself with *practice* as opposed to 'aims and objectives' in *School-Based Staff Development Activities: A Handbook for Secondary Schools* by D. Oldroyd, K. Smith and J. Lee, Longman for the Schools Council (1984).
3 There's an interesting example of a History department building policy through the children in *Curriculum 11–16: Towards a Statement of Entitlement*, HMI (1983), pp. 42–3 published by DES.
4 *The English Department Book*, published by the ILEA English Centre, (1982), has an excellent section (one of many) on assessment and profiling (pp. 95–103).
5 6 June 1983.
6 'Broken English' by Keith Kimberly, *The Times Educational Supplement*, 10 February 1984.
7 *Saville* by David Storey, Penguin edition p. 279.

6 Micros and English

A short section of this chapter has been adopted from an article written jointly with Joan Ashton, published under the title 'Sense of Responsibility' in *The Times Educational Supplement* of May 25th 1984.
1 The *Guardian* article, 'The Mind Blowing Experiences' (12 January 1984), was an edited extract from a new foreword to *Computer Power and Human Reason*, Penguin (1984).
2 *Exploring English with Microcomputers*, ed. D. Chandler, Council for Educational Technology NATE (1983).
3 *Computer World* magazine, quoted in *The Third Wave* by Alvin Toffler, Pan (1981).
4 Now commercially available from CLASS. (Cambridge Language Arts Software Services.)
5 *The Third Wave*, op. cit., p. 184.

7 English with Drama?

1 Gavin Bolton – author of *Towards a Theory of Drama in Education*, Longman (1979) – is Lecturer in Drama-in-Education at Durham University.
2 Where a description of a situation or a character sketch is written out on a piece of card.
3 A Tableau is like a photograph: a group establishes the positions as if caught by the camera and then moves out from that frozen movement through action and dialogue.
4 When a teacher assumes a character within the drama lesson.
5 *Dorothy Heathcote: Collected Writings on Education and Drama*, ed. L. Johnson and C. O'Neill, Hutchinson (1984).

8 Making decisions in a changing world

1 *Microelectronics in Teaching and Learning* by N. E. Trowbridge, Hampshire Education Department (1979).
2 It was Matthew Arnold! From *The Oxford Book of Literary Anecdotes*: the speaker is Lina Waterfield in *Castle in Italy: an autobiography*, Murray (1961).

Appendix 1:
Associations and
Contacts

- *Schools' Poetry Association*
  Twyford School, Winchester, Hampshire, SO21 1NW.
- *ATCAL (Association for the Teaching of Caribbean, African and Associated Literature)*
  Membership (individual/institutional): The National Treasurer, 138 Shaftesbury Avenue, Kenton, Middlesex. Also can be contacted through the Africa Centre, 38 King Street, London WC2E 8JT. Tel. 01–836 1973.
- *Women's Education Group*
  Publishes *Gen*, an anti-sexist educational journal. Women's Education Resource Centre, ILEA Drama and Tape Centre, Princeton Street, London WC1.
- *Educational Foundation for Visual Aids (EFVA)*
  254 Belsize Road, London NW6 4BY.
- *The English Centre* (ILEA)
  Sutherland Street, London SW1
- *National Association for the Teaching of English (NATE)*
  49 Broomgrove Road, Sheffield S10 2NA.
- *The Arvon Foundation (Totleigh Barton Writing Courses)*
  Totleigh Barton, Sheepwash, Beaworthy, Devon EX21 5NS. Tel. Black Torrington 338.
- *United Kingdom Reading Association (UKRA)*
  c/o Edge Hill College of Education, St Helens Road, Ormskirk, Lancs.
- *National Book League (NBL)*
  Book exhibitions. Book House, 45 East Hill, Wandsworth, London SW18 2HZ. Tel. 01–870 9055/8.
- *British Film Institute (BFI)*
  81 Dean Street, London W1V 6AA. Tel. 01–437 4355.

- *Writers in Schools*
  Contact your local Regional Arts Association.
- *Poetry Society*
  National Poetry Centre, 21 Earls Court Square, London SW5.

Appendix 2: Recommended books on the teaching of English

General
- *The English Department Book*, ILEA English Centre (1982).
- *A Language For Life*, HMSO (1975).
- *Best Laid Plans: English Teachers at Work*, ed. S. Horner, Longman for the Schools Council (1983).
- *English Teaching Since 1965 – How much Growth?*, David Allen, Heinemann (1980).
- *New Directions in English Teaching*, A. Adams, Falmer Press (1982).
- *English Studies 11–18: An Arts Based Approach*, ed. B. Harrison, Hodder & Stoughton (1983).
- *Continuity in Secondary English*, D. Jackson, Methuen (1982).
- *Teaching English: A Linguistic Approach*, J. Keen, Methuen (1978).
- *English Within the Arts*, Peter Abbs, Hodder & Stoughton (1982).
- *Growth through English*, J. Dixon, Oxford University Press (1967).
- *Versions of English*, D. Barnes, D. Barnes and S. Clarke, Heinemann (1984).
- *Guidelines for English 13–16*, County of Avon Education Department (1981).

Reading
- *Learning to Read*, M. Meek, The Bodley Head (1982).
- *Reading*, F. Smith, Cambridge University Press (1978).
- *Developing Response to Fiction*, R Protherough, Open University Press (1983).
- *Children, Language and Literature: An In-service Pack for Teachers*, Open University (1982).
- *The Effective Use of Reading*, ed. E. Lunzer and K. Gardner, Heinemann (1979).

- *Achieving Literacy*, M. Meek, Routledge & Kegan Paul (1983).
- *Encounters with Books: Teaaching Fiction 11–16*, D. Jackson, Methuen (1983).
- *A Handbook for Teaching African Literature*, E. Gunner, Heinemann (1984).
- *Working with Fiction*, M. Hayhoe and S. Parker, Arnold (1984).
- *Books and Reading Development*, Jennie Ingham, Heinemann (1981).
- *The Good Book Guide to Children's Books*, ed. B. Taylor and P. Braithwaite, Penguin (1984).
- *The Signal Review of Children's Books 1 and 2*, ed. A. Chambers, Thimble Press (1983/4).
- *Fiction as a Starting Point for Learning 8–14*
                                Wakefield Literature and Learning Project (1983).
- *Some Uses of Role Play as an Approach to the Study of Fiction 8–14*

Writing
- *Draft Writing in English*, Cleveland English Curriculum Paper 1.
- *Learning through Writing*, Bernard Harrison, NFER/Nelson (1983).
- *Writing and the Writer*, F. Smith, Heinemann (1982).
- *Writing: Teachers and Children at Work*, Donald Graves, Heinemann (1983).
- *Opportunities for Writing at 17+*, Schools Council English 16–19 Project.
- *Coursework in English*, ed. P. Scott, Longman for the Schools Council (1983).
- *Encouraging Writing*, R. Protherough, Methuen (1983).
- *Whatever comes to mind: an experiment in journal writing*, K. Eames, 'Learning about Learning' booklet 3, Wiltshire Education Department (1982).

Talk
See also the language section below.
- *Becoming Our Own Experts*, Talk Workshop Group, ILEA English Centre (1982).
- *Encouraging Talk*, L. Knowles, Methuen (1983).

Language
- *Language Across the Transition*, M. Creasey, F. Findlay and B. Walsh, Longman for the Schools Council (1983).
- *Lost For Words*, P. Creber, Penguin (1972).
- *Inside Classrooms* (Vol. 2), ed. M. Wilson, Bulmershe College, Reading (1983).
- *Language Policies in Action*, ed. M. Torbe, Ward Lock (1980).
- *Language Perspectives*, ed. B. Wade. Heinemann (1982).
- *Language Across the Curriculum*, ed. M. Marland, Heinemann (1977).

Evaluation

- *Mark My Words*, T. Dunsbee and T. Ford, Ward Lock/NATE (1980).
- *English: Teachers and the Examination Boards*, NATE (1983).
- *Alternatives at English A level*, NATE (1983).
- *Assessment in a Multicultural Society: English at 16+*, L. Fallows, Longman for the Schools Council (1983).
- *Evaluating the English Department*, D. Allen, Evaluation in Education (1983).

Micros

- *Exploring English with Microcomputers*, ed. D. Chandler, CET/NATE (1983).
- *Mindstorms: Children, Computers and Powerful Ideas*, S. Papert, Harvester (1980).
- *Teaching Humanities in the Microelectronic Age*, A. Adams and E. Jones, Open University Press (1983).
- 'Tomorrow, and Tomorrow, and Tomorrow', (article), B. Robinson, in *English in Education*, spring 1984.

Drama

- *Dorothy Heathcote: Collected Writings on Education and Drama*, ed. L. Johnson and C. O'Neill, Hutchinson (1984).
- *Towards a Theory of Drama in Education*, Gavin Bolton, Longman (1979).
- *Drama as Context*, D. Heathcote, NATE (1980).
- *New Directions in Drama Teaching*, ed. M. Wootton, Heinemann (1982).
- *Learning through Drama*, L. McGregor, M. Tate and K. Robinson, Heinemann (1977).
- *The Arts in Schools*, Calouste Gulbenkian (1980).
- *Dramastarters*, G. Stoate, Harrap (1984).
- *Theatre Games*, C. Barker, Eyre Methuen (1977).
- *Drama Structures*, C. O'Neill and A. Lambert, Hutchinson (1982).
- *Impro*, K. Johnstone, Eyre Methuen (1981).
- *Drama Guidelines*, C. O'Neill and A. Lambert, R. Linnell and J. Warr-Wood, Heinemann in association with London Drama (1976).
- *Plays for Young People to Read and Perform*, Aidan Chambers, Thimble Press (1982).

Other

- *Debate and Decision: Schools in a World of Change*, World Studies Project (1980) – useful for in-service ideas.

- *English in the 1980s: a programme of support for teachers*, Schools Council Paper 62.
- *Alternatives in Education at 16–19: English – a case study*, A. Adams and T. Hopkin, Blackie (1981).
- *Teaching Spelling*, M. Torbe, Ward Lock (1976).
- *Teaching about Television*, L. Masterman, Macmillan (1980).

Appendix 3: Recommended Fiction

Lower School

The Broken Saddle,	James Aldridge	Julia MacRae Books
Blubber,	Judy Blume	Piccolo
The Eighteenth Emergency,	Betsy Byars	Puffin
The Midnight Fox,	Betsy Byars	Puffin
Ghost After Ghost,	ed. Aidan Chambers	Kestrel
The Dark Behind the Curtain,	Gillian Cross	Oxford
Conrad's War,	Andrew Davies	Hippo
Grinny,	Nicholas Fisk	Puffin
Fair's Fair,	Leon Garfield	Macdonald
The Shrinking of Treehorn,	Florence Parry Heide	Puffin
The Mouse and his Child,	Russell Hoban	Puffin
How Tom Beat Captain Najork and the Hired Sportsmen,	Russell Hoban	Jonathan Cape
The Iron Man,	Ted Hughes	Faber
The Turbulent Term of Tike Tiler	Gene Kemp	Puffin
Gowie Corby Plays Chicken,	Gene Kemp	Puffin
Charlie Lewis Plays for Time,	Gene Kemp	Faber
Dog Days and Cat Naps,	Gene Kemp	Puffin
The Clock Tower Ghost,	Gene Kemp	Puffin
The Ghost of Thomas Kempe,	Penelope Lively	Puffin
Goodnight Mister Tom,	Michelle Magorian	Puffin
The Haunting,	Margaret Mahy	Dent
Thunder and Lightnings,	Jan Mark	Puffin
Hairs in the Palm of the Hand,	Jan Mark	Puffin
Nothing to be Afraid of,	Jan Mark	Puffin
Summer of the Zeppelin,	Elsie McCutcheon	Dent/ Puffin

Not Now Bernard,	David McKee	Andersen Press
The Goalkeeper's Revenge,	Bill Naughton	Puffin
Mrs Frisby and the Rats of Nimh,	Robert O'Brien	Puffin
Playing Beatie Bow,	Ruth Park	Puffin
Jacob Have I Loved,	Katherine Paterson	Puffin
A Bridge to Terabithia,	Katherine Paterson	Puffin
Battle of Bubble and Squeak,	Philippa Pearce	Puffin
The Dream Time,	Henry Treece	Brockhampton Press
Hi There, Supermouse,	Jean Ure	Hutchinson
Charlotte's Web,	E. B. White	Puffin

Middle school

The Trouble with Donovan Croft	Bernard Ashley	Puffin
Joby,	Stan Barstow	New Windmill
Carrie's War,	Nina Bawden	Puffin
Tales of a Fourth Grade Nothing,	Judy Blume	Piccolo
Comeback,	Marjorie Drake	Kestrel
A Question of Courage,	Marjorie Darke	Lions
East End at Your Feet,	Farrukh Dhondy	Macmillan Topliners
Black Jack,	Leon Garfield	Puffin
The Friends,	Rosa Guy	Puffin
Dinky Hocker Shoots Smack!,	M. E. Kerr	New Windmill
A Separate Peace,	John Knowles	New Windmill
Harold and Bella, Jammy and Me	Robert Leeson	Fontana Lions
Silver's Revenge,	Robert Leeson	Collins
A Fine Boy for Killing,	Jan Needle	Deutsch
Z for Zachariah,	Robert O'Brien	New Windmill
The Great Gilly Hopkins,	Katherine Paterson	Puffin
Fireweed,	Jill Paton Walsh	Puffin
The Pigman,	Paul Zindel	Fontana Lions

Upper school

| *Tiger Eyes,* | Judy Blume | New Windmill |
| *Dance on My Grave,* | Aidan Chambers | Bodley Head |

The Chocolate War,	Robert Cormier	Fontana Lions
I Am the Cheese,	Robert Cormier	Fontana Lions
Healer,	Peter Dickinson	Gollancz
Welcome to Hard Times,	E. L. Doctorow	Pan
Nobody's Family is Going to Change,	L. Fitzhugh	Fontana Lions
Looks and Smiles,	Barry Hines	Penguin
Collision Course,	N. Hinton	Puffin Plus
The Damned,	Linda Hoy	Bodley Head
Basketball Game,	Julius Lester	Puffin Plus
Across the Barricades,	Joan Lingard	Puffin Plus
12th Day of July,	Joan Lingard	Puffin Plus
A Summer to Die,	Lois Lowry	Kestrel
Feet,	Jan Mark	Kestrel
Southerly Buster,	Christobel Mattingley	Hodder & Stoughton
Piggy in the Middle,	Jan Needle	Fontana Lions
A Midsummer Night's Death,	K. M. Peyton	Puffin Plus
The Wave,	Morton Rhue	Puffin Plus
The Catcher in the Rye,	J. D. Salinger	Penguin
The Secret Diary of Adrian Mole,	Sue Townsend	Methuen
There is a Happy Land,	Keith Waterhouse	Longman
The Machine Gunners,	Robert Westall	Puffin
The Scarecrows,	Robert Westall	Puffin Plus
A Girl Who Wanted a Boy,	Paul Zindel	Puffin

'Short stories'

'The Pedestrian', Ray Bradbury

'Harry', Rosemary Timperley, in *Could It Be?*

'The Breadwinner', Leslie Halward, in *Storymakers*

'Indian Camp', 'The End of Something', 'Ten Indians', Ernest Hemingway

'The Great Leapfrog Contest', William Saroyan

'The Sniper', Liam O'Flaherty, in *Loves, Hopes and Fears*

'Hallmarked', Walter Macken, in *Loves, Hopes and Fears*

'Spit Nolan', 'Boozer's Labourer', 'Late Night on Watling Street', '17 Oranges', Bill Naughton

'Manhood', John Wain, in *Story* Penguin

'The Leaping Lad', Sid Chaplin

'The Destructors', Graham Greene

'The Search for Tommy Flynn', Stan Barstow

'My Oedipus Complex' Frank O'Connor

'Examination Day', Henry Slessor, in *Storylines*

'Their Mother's Purse', Walter Macken, in *Loves, Hopes and Fears*

'The One Who Waits', Ray Bradbury, in *Other Worlds*, Penguin English
  Project 1.

'Death A Prisoner', Fritz Muller-Guggenbuhl, in *Other Worlds*, op. cit.

'KBW', Farrukh Dhondy, in *East End at Your Feet*

'Tomorrow and Tomorrow and So Forth', John Updike, in *The Same
  Door*, Penguin

'Posts and Telecommunications', Jan Mark, in *Feet*

'The Place', Ray Bradbury

'Vendetta', Guy de Maupassant

'The Parsley Garden', William Saroyan

'Nothing to be Afraid of', Jan Mark in *Nothing to be Afraid of.*

'The Gatewood Caper', Dashiel Hammett

Appendix 4: Poetry That 'Works'

Blake, William 'A Poison Tree', in *Voices 2*, Penguin (1968)

Brownjohn, Alan 'We're Going to see the Rabbit', in *The New Dragon Book of Verse*, Oxford University Press (1977)

Causley, Charles 'The Ballad of Charlotte Dymond' in *Collected Poems*, Macmillan

Causley, Charles 'Miller's End', in *Telescope*, Arnold (1974)

Cohen, Leonard 'Warning', in *Poems 1956–68*, Jonathan Cape (1969)

Connor, Tony 'Hilltop and Guy Fawkes', in *Telescope* op. cit.

Cummings, E.E. 'ygUDuh', in *Selected Poems 1923–1958*, Penguin (1963)

Fenton, James 'The Skip', in *The Memory of War*, Penguin (1984)

Frost, Robert 'Out, Out', in *Selected Poems*, Penguin (1955)

Harrison, Tony 'Long Distance II', in *Selected Poems*, Penguin (1984)

Heaney, Seamus 'Bye Child', in *Selected Poems 1965–1975*, Faber (1980)

Heaney, Seamus 'Midterm Break', in *Selected Poems* , op. cit.

Hesketh, Phoebe 'Geriatric Ward', in *Themes: Generations*, Heinemann Education (1972)

Hurst, John 'End of A Harvest Day', in *Every Man Will Shout*, Oxford University Press (1964)

Jones, Brian 'The Day We Moved To Greenford', in *Themes: Town and Country*, Heinemann Education (1972)

King, Denise 'The Funeral of Father', in *City Lines*, ILEA English Centre (1982)

Lochead, Liz 'The Choosing', in *Strictly Private*, Puffin

Lucie-Smith, Edward 'The Lesson', in *Penguin Modern Poets 6*, Penguin (1964)

Macbeth, George 'The Bird', in *Touchstones 3*, Hodder and Stoughton (1969)

MacCaig, Norman 'Interruption to a Journey', in *Themes: Town and Country*, op. cit.

MacLean, Alasdair 'Death of an old Woman', in *Telescope*, op. cit.

Masters, Lee Edgar 'Butch Weldy', in *Every Man Will Shout*, op. cit.

Norris, Leslie 'The Ballad of Billy Rose', in *Encounters*, Longman (1965)

Patten, Brian 'Song for Last Year's Wife', in *Love, Love, Love*, Corgi (1967)

Porter, Peter 'Your Attention Please', in *Collected Poems*, Oxford University Press (1983)

Raine, Craig 'A Martian Sends a Postcard Home', in *A Martian Sends a Postcard Home*, Oxford University Press (1979)

Raine, Craig 'A Hungry Fighter', in *Rich*, Faber (1984)

Scannell, Vernon 'Dead Dog', in *Telescope*, op. cit.

Scannell, Vernon 'Autobiographical Note', in *Touchstones 3*, op. cit.

Snyder, Gary 'Hay for the Horses', in *Voices 3*, Penguin

Souster, Raymond 'The Man Who Finds that His Son Has Become a Thief', in *Themes: Conflict*, Heinemann (1969

Stafford, William 'Travelling Through the Dark', in *Voices 2*, op. cit.

Stallworthy, Jon 'The Trap', in *Themes: Imagination*, Heinemann

Sutton, David 'Starlings', in *Dragonsteeth*, Arnold (1972)

Thien, Ho 'Green Beret', (see pages 23–24 above)

Turner, Steve 'Daily London Recipe', in *Tonight We Will Fake Love*, Charisma (1974), Razor (1976)

Walsh, John 'The Bully Asleep', in *Touchstones 3*. op. cit.

Wright, Kit 'The Rovers', in *Hot Dog and other Poems*, Kestrel (1981)

In addition, the following are useful background:

Poetry in the Making by Ted Hughes, Faber (1967); *NATEPACK 1: Poetry*, NATE (1984); *Pupil, Teacher, Poem* by Peter Benton, Hodder & Stoughton (1985); *The RattleBag*, ed. Seamus Heaney and Ted Hughes, Faber (1982); *Does it Have to Rhyme?* by Sandy Brownjohn, Hodder & Stoughton (1980), and *What Rhymes with Secret?*, by the same author, (1982). There is an excellent list of anthologies in 'Poetry in the Secondary School' by B. Harrison in *English Studies 11–18*, Hodder & Stoughton (1983).

Appendix 5: Fifty Non-Sexist Books for Use in the Secondary School

This list was compiled by Joanna Roberts (Langtree School, Woodcote, Oxfordshire); it draws on a variety of sources: *The Spare Rib List of Non-Sexist Books*; Bob Dixon's book *Catching them Young: Sex, Race and Class in Children's Fiction*; an ILEA list (English Centre) and recommendations from many teachers of English.

Section 1: Class readers
Break in the Sun, Bernard Ashley, Oxford (1980)/Puffin (1981)
The Eyes of the Amaryllis, Natalie Babbitt, Chatto (1977)
Tuck Everlasting, Natalie Babbitt, Chatto and Windus (1977)
The Eighteenth Emergency, Betsy Byars, Bodley Head (1974)/Puffin (1976)
The Midnight Fox, Betsy Byars, Faber 1970/Puffin (1976)
The Pinballs, Betsy Byars, Bodley Head (1977) Puffin
The Winter of the Birds, Helen Cresswell, Faber 1975/Puffin (1979)
A Long Way to Go, Marjorie Darke, Puffin (1982)
The Devil's Children, Peter Dickinson, Puffin (1982)
Harriet the Spy, Louise Fitzhugh, Fontana/Lions (1975)
Julie of the Wolves, Jean Craighead George, Puffin (1976)
The Turbulent Term of Tike Tiler, Gene Kemp, Faber (1977)/Puffin (1979)
Gowie Corby Plays Chicken, Gene Kemp, Faber (1979) Puffin (1981)
When Hitler Stole Pink Rabbit, Judith Kerr, Fontana/Lions (1974)
It's My Life, Robert Leeson, Fontana/Lions (1981)
12th Day of July, Joan Lingard, Puffin (1973)
Across the Barricades, Joan Lingard, Hamish Hamilton (1972) Puffin (1973)

Hairs in the Palm of the Hand, Jan Mark, Kestrel (1981)/Puffin (1983)
Conrad-the-factory-made-boy, Christine Nostlinger, Beaver Target (1976)
Z for Zachariah, Robert O'Brien, Gollancz (1975)/New Windmill (1976)
The Great Gilly Hopkins, Katherine Paterson, Puffin (1981)
That Crazy April, Lila Perl, Collins/Fontana (1978)
Letty, Avril Rowlands, Puffin (1984)
Underground to Canada, Barbara Smucker, Puffin (1978)
Josh, Ivan Southall, Angus and Robertson (1971) Puffin (1973)
Roll of Thunder, Hear My Cry, Mildred Taylor, Gollancz (1977)
The Practical Princess and other Liberating Fairytales, Jay Williams, Scholastic/Chatto (1983)
The Pigman, Paul Zindel, Bodley Head (1969) Macmillan Fontana Lions (1976)

Section 2: Individual readers
Huck and Her Time Machine, Gillian Avery, Collins (1977) Lions
One More River, Lynne Reid Banks, Puffin (1980)
Mia, Gunnel Beckman, Longman Knockouts (1976)
The Fox in Winter, John Branfield, Gollancz (1980) Fontana (1981)
Tiger Eyes, Judy Blume, New Windmill (1984)
The Whys and Wherefores of Littabelle Lea, Vera and Bill Cleaver, Hamish Hamilton (1974)
A Question of Courage, Marjorie Darke, Kestrel (1975) Fontana/Lions (1978)
Charlotte Sometimes, Penelope Farmer, Chatto (1969) Puffin (1972)
Nobody's Family is Going to Change, Louise Fitzhugh, Gollancz/Lions
Watch all Night, John Foster, Puffin (1980)
Blowfish Live in the Sea, Paula Fox, Puffin (1974)
Summer of My German Soldier, Bette Greene, Puffin (1977)
Pappa Pellerin's Daughter, Maria Gripe, Chatto (1966)
The Friends, Rosa Guy, Gollancz (1973)
Hey Dollface, Deborah Hautzig, Fontana (1982)
Second Star to the Right, Deborah Hautzig, Puffin (1982)
From the Mixed up Files of Mrs Basil E. Frankweiler, E. L. Konigsburg, Macmillan (1969)
A Summer to Die, Lois Lowry, Kestrel (1977)
Bridge to Terabithia, Katherine Paterson, Gollancz (1982)/Puffin (1980)
Freaky Friday, Mary Rodgers, Hamish Hamilton (1973)/Puffin (1976)
Let the Circle Be Unbroken, Mildred D. Taylor, Gollancz (1982)/Puffin

Index